'A collection of witty es   . . .
What will survive of La   s a
joyful immersion in it. 1   on
the best poet of his lifetii   les

'The brilliance of James's ɩ   ᵤ...ᵤ view of Larkin's
solitude and humanity, anu ɩne fragile friendship between the two
recorded in the book's final pages, provide a monument to human
connection and isolation together'

Andrew Hunter Murray, *Guardian*

'This slim collection of Clive James's writings on Philip Larkin demon-
strates both a life-long passion for the poet's work and a deep critical
endeavour to rehabilitate his reputation as one of the greatest poets
of the 20th century. A collection to savour two-fold – for the genius
of Larkin and the playful erudition of James'

Carl Wilkinson, *Financial Times*, Best Books of 2019

'To read a major critic on a major poet is one of the great pleasures.
Clive James's passion for the work of Philip Larkin, his intense scrutiny which reveals an extraordinary empathy makes *Somewhere
Becoming Rain: Collected Writings on Philip Larkin* an outstanding
book'   Melvyn Bragg, *New Statesman*, Books of the Year 2019

'This is a tribute to Larkin's poems. James is good at reminding us
why and how they were powerful, multivalent and memorable . . .
He is also unusually observant. His parallels between Larkin and
Montale are elucidating'   Rory Waterman, *TLS*

'James's criticism is a constant delight, since it arises always from
unprescriptive reading and rereading . . . Insights of this quality are
rare, and we get more than our fair share of them in this volume'

James Booth, *The Critic*

Somewhere Becoming Rain

Clive James was the multi-million-copy bestselling author of more than forty books. His poetry collection *Sentenced to Life* and his translation of Dante's *The Divine Comedy* were both *Sunday Times* top-ten bestsellers, and his collections of verse were shortlisted for many prizes. In 2012 he was appointed CBE and in 2013 an Officer of the Order of Australia. He died in 2019.

ALSO BY CLIVE JAMES

AUTOBIOGRAPHY

Unreliable Memoirs · Falling Towards England
May Week Was In June · North Face of Soho
The Blaze of Obscurity

FICTION

Brilliant Creatures · The Remake
Brrm! Brrm! · The Silver Castle

VERSE

Other Passports: Poems 1958–1985
The Book of My Enemy: Collected Verse 1958–2003
Opal Sunset: Selected Poems 1958–2008
Angels Over Elsinore: Collected Verse 2003–2008
Nefertiti in the Flak Tower · Sentenced to Life
Collected Poems 1958–2015 · Gate of Lilacs
Injury Time · The River in the Sky

TRANSLATION

The Divine Comedy

CRITICISM

The Metropolitan Critic (new edition, 1994)
Visions Before Midnight · The Crystal Bucket
First Reactions (US) *· From the Land of Shadows*
Glued to the Box · Snakecharmers in Texas
The Dreaming Swimmer · Fame in the 20th Century
On Television · Even As We Speak · Reliable Essays
As of This Writing (US) *· The Meaning of Recognition*
Cultural Amnesia · The Revolt of the Pendulum
A Point of View · Poetry Notebook · The Fire of Joy

TRAVEL

Flying Visits

CLIVE JAMES

Somewhere Becoming Rain

Collected Writings on Philip Larkin

PICADOR

First published 2019 by Picador

This paperback edition first published 2021 by Picador
an imprint of Pan Macmillan
The Smithson, 6 Briset Street, London EC1M 5NR
EU representative: Macmillan Publishers Ireland Ltd, 1st Floor,
The Liffey Trust Centre, 117–126 Sheriff Street Upper,
Dublin 1, D01 YC43
Associated companies throughout the world
www.panmacmillan.com

ISBN 978-1-5290-2885-0

1 3 5 7 9 8 6 4 2

A CIP catalogue record for this book is available from the British Library.

Typeset in Minion Pro by Palimpsest Book Production Limited,
Falkirk, Stirlingshire
Printed and bound by CPI Group (UK) Ltd, Croydon, CR0 4YY

Visit **www.picador.com** to read more about all our books
and to buy them. You will also find features, author interviews and
news of any author events, and you can sign up for e-newsletters
so that you're always first to hear about our new releases.

To Claerwen, who saw
that these pieces ought to be a book

Contents

Introduction

The arrangement of this book might seem episodic at first but it was lamentably true that Philip Larkin, who threw a tall shadow by the time of his death, was nevertheless obliged to die by inches, with fist-fights raging in the graveyard. I wish the battle had been fought and won, and his soul might rest easy. But the struggle continues. People of surprisingly high intelligence have managed to convince themselves that Larkin's poetry didn't amount to much at all. And presumably, to them, it doesn't, although their dismissal of him makes you wonder whose poetry they think does matter, if his does not. Sometimes they tell us, and we think that he has had a lucky escape. But it might have been an escape all the way to oblivion, if the total audience for poetry had been easier to persuade.

Luckily it was not, and the true story behind this episodic book is the gradual but unstoppable increase of his prestige as it grew to match the common reader's love. He was just an ordinary man – too often he thought of himself as even less than that – but behind his show of diffidence (he was still on the threshold of a stammer even at the end) there was a highly developed sense of duty to his gift. Indeed that sense of duty shaped his life, sometimes to the point of distortion. Would he really have put such ingenuity and effort into hoodwinking the several women who loved him if he had not realised that his need for affection was matched by an equally consuming need to be alone?

And being alone meant being alone with the next piece of writing, even when it was just a column about a few jazz discs that he privately thought should be left in front of the two-bar radiator until they melted. When the next piece of writing was a poem (sometimes a poem that had been in the works for years) nothing else counted. Nothing was going to take his attention away from those few lines that were searching for the paths by which they could become a few more, or even just one more, or even – enough sweat for tonight – no more.

He was trained up for it. At the end of this book we will find the great double origin of his gift for creative solitude. If the letters to and from his father do not precisely reveal the old man as the Nazi sympathiser that Larkin's detractors are still hopefully expecting to take the stage, they do reveal that Larkin's father blessed him with a long close-up of what it looked and sounded like to be concerned with English grammar and its correct usage; and his mother emerges as the great analyst of the grocer's shop shelves who shared and helped to shape his taste for the commonplace. Here is the chance for the reader, especially the male reader, to overcome his Hemingway complex. The chances are that he won't spend much of his future diving out of an aircraft and sprinting into battle. More likely he will be hovering between the supermarket display cases checking out the rising price of Marmite. Larkin's mother gave her stammering son the assurance to find his way through the ticketed maze, and his father gave him the precision of language to shape what he remembered.

All we need to remember, when it comes to the appreciation of his mental discipline, is that his creative solitude was achieved in company, with no duty shirked. Though it is hard to imagine him looking forward to a meeting of the library car-park-space allocation committee, or whatever grim task loomed next, it is equally impossible to imagine him ducking out of it. Bohemia is a refuge, and he never stepped towards it even once, except perhaps in that short period at Oxford when he sported a cravat. The everyday might have been full of things that he found dull, but the everyday was his subject. We need to be very confident about our own everyday before we find his unexciting. In that respect, we should be cautious about joining him in his critical remarks about his owlish glasses. All the evidence – and most of it is in his poetry – suggests that he could hear the fizz when light hit the window. The times when he seems to complain about being less than blessed are the very times when we should remember that he was more than human, with powers of registration verging on the divine.

When Larkin seems set on being even more miserable than T. S. Eliot about the paucity of events while walking in a country lane, it's important to remember that Larkin might be seeing even more than his great predecessor, and certainly seeing more than us. His powers of sensitive discrimination went all the way down to the syntax. 'Or not untrue and not unkind'. The drama was in the shadings of the grammar. It follows that we need to pay close attention to the way he writes things down. My chief secretary on this project, the novelist Deborah Meyler, is still convinced that Larkin, in the celebrated last few lines of the poem 'High Windows', is painting a picture not of desolation, but of richness. ('. . . the deep blue air, that shows/ Nothing, and is nowhere, and is endless.') She thinks there is hope in that. I myself think that there is no more hope in that than there is in a human body about to hit the ground after a long fall, but to convince her of her misapprehension all I can do is go on quoting Larkin at her, and I noticed long ago that her memory for his lines is even better than mine. (I only thought that I could remember every line he wrote, but it turned out that she really can.) Our struggle for supremacy will probably culminate on a slated roof, with a body falling to the gleaming street below. A matter of life and death? No: a lot more serious than that.

My other secretary, Susie Young, is present in the text more as a site-supervisor than a critic of detail, but her sane influence is still palpable throughout. Without her computer skills I would have been lost in the jungle. The influence of my elder daughter Claerwen James, who had the idea of collecting these pieces, is constantly present in the text as a bulwark against rhetorical excess. She also designed the jacket, which to my mind turns Hull into the magic city that Larkin clearly had in mind when he wrote those beautiful lines about the sunlight draining down the estuary. My wife Prue Shaw keeps up with everything I write, just in case I am showing signs too flagrant of having finally gone berserk. Luckily, however, Larkin's complete works, still accumulating with the help of scholarship, are a calming influence. One wants, after all, to be as cool and clear as he was. It isn't like dealing with the kind of poet who can't talk sense to save his life. Apart from the very occasional poem that might be classified as deliberately obscure, every Larkin creation makes nothing but sense on the level of straightforward statement; and then, even more remarkably, it goes on being intelligible as it climbs into the realms of implication, until finally there you are, up above the estuary and heading down a cloudy channel towards where? Well, nowhere except everywhere.

Cambridge, 2019

Somewhere Becoming Rain

PHILIP LARKIN, *COLLECTED POEMS*
EDITED BY ANTHONY THWAITE
(FABER, 1988)

At first glance, the publication in the United States of Philip Larkin's *Collected Poems* looks like a long shot. While he lived, Larkin never crossed the Atlantic. Unlike some other British poets, he was genuinely indifferent to his American reputation. His bailiwick was England. Larkin was so English that he didn't even care much about Britain, and he rarely mentioned it. Even within England, he travelled little. He spent most of his adult life at the University of Hull, as its chief librarian. A trip to London was an event. When he was there, he resolutely declined to promote his reputation. He guarded it but would permit no hype.

Though Larkin's diffidence was partly a pose, his reticence was authentic. At no point did he announce that he had built a better mousetrap. The world had to prove it by beating a path to his door. The process took time, but was inexorable, and by now, only three years after his death, at the age of sixty-three, it has reached a kind of apotheosis. On the British bestseller lists, Larkin's *Collected Poems* was up there for months at a stretch, along with Stephen Hawking's *A Brief History of Time* and Salman Rushdie's *The Satanic Verses*. In Larkin's case, this extraordinary level of attention was reached without either general relativity's having to be reconciled with quantum mechanics or the Ayatollah Khomeini's being required to pronounce anathema. The evidence suggests that Larkin's poetry, from a standing start, gets to everyone capable of being got to. One's tender concern that it should survive the perilous journey across the sea is therefore perhaps misplaced. A mission like this might have no more need of a fighter escort than pollen on the wind.

The size of the volume is misleading. Its meticulous editor,

Anthony Thwaite – himself a poet of high reputation – has included poems that Larkin finished but did not publish, and poems that he did not even publish. Though tactfully carried out, this editorial inclusiveness is not beyond cavil. What was elliptically concentrated has become more fully understandable, but whether Larkin benefits from being more fully understood is a poser. Eugenio Montale, in many ways a comparable figure, was, it might be recalled, properly afraid of what he called 'too much light'.

During his lifetime, Larkin published only three mature collections of verse, and they were all as thin as blades. *The Less Deceived* (1955), *The Whitsun Weddings* (1964), and *High Windows* (1974) combined to a thickness barely half that of the *Collected Poems*. Larkin also published, in 1966, a new edition of his early, immature collection, *The North Ship*, which had first come out in 1945. He took care, by supplying the reissue with a deprecatory introduction, to keep it clearly separate from the poems that he regarded as being written in his own voice.

The voice was unmistakable. It made misery beautiful. One of Larkin's few even halfway carefree poems is 'For Sidney Bechet', from *The Whitsun Weddings*. Yet the impact that Larkin said Bechet made on him was exactly the impact that Larkin made on readers coming to him for the first time:

> On me your voice falls as they say love should,
> Like an enormous yes.

What made the paradox delicious was the scrupulousness of its expression. There could be no doubt that Larkin's outlook on life added up to an enormous no, but pessimism had been given a saving grace. Larkin described an England changing in ways he didn't like. The empire had shrunk to a few islands, his personal history to a set of missed opportunities. Yet his desperate position, which ought logically to have been a licence for incoherence, was expressed with such linguistic fastidiousness on the one hand and such lyrical enchantment on the other that the question arose of whether he had not at least partly cultivated that view in order to get those results.

Larkin once told an interviewer, 'Deprivation for me is what daffodils were for Wordsworth.'

In the three essential volumes, the balanced triad of Larkin's achievement, all the poems are poised vibrantly in the force field of tension between his profound personal hopelessness and the assured command of their carrying out. Perfectly designed, tightly integrated, making the feeling of falling apart fit together, they release, from their compressed but always strictly parsable syntax, sudden phrases of ravishing beauty, as the river in Dante's Paradise suggests by giving off sparks that light is what it is made of.

These irresistible fragments are everyone's way into Larkin's work. They are the first satisfaction his poetry offers. There are other and deeper satisfactions, but it was his quotability that gave Larkin the biggest cultural impact on the British reading public since Auden – and over a greater social range. Lines by Larkin are the common property of everyone in Britain who reads seriously at all – a state of affairs which has not obtained since the time of Tennyson. Phrases, whole lines, and sometimes whole stanzas can be heard at the dinner table.

> There is an evening coming in
> Across the fields, one never seen before,
> That lights no lamps . . .

> Only one ship is seeking us, a black-
> Sailed unfamiliar, towing at her back
> A huge and birdless silence. In her wake
> No waters breed or break . . .

> Now, helpless in the hollow of
> An unarmorial age, a trough
> Of smoke in slow suspended skeins
> Above their scrap of history,
> Only an attitude remains . . .

And as the tightened brakes took hold, there swelled
A sense of falling, like an arrow-shower
Sent out of sight, somewhere becoming rain . . .

How distant, the departure of young men
Down valleys, or watching
The green shore past the salt-white cordage
Rising and falling . . .

Steep beach, blue water, towels, red bathing caps,
The small hushed waves' repeated fresh collapse
Up the warm yellow sand, and further off
A white steamer stuck in the afternoon . . .

Later, the square is empty: a big sky
Drains down the estuary like the bed
Of a gold river . . .

At death, you break up: the bits that were you
Start speeding away from each other for ever
With no one to see . . .

Rather than words comes the thought of high windows:
The sun-comprehending glass,
And beyond it, the deep blue air, that shows
Nothing, and is nowhere, and is endless.

Drawn in by the subtle gravity beam of such bewitchment, the reader
becomes involved for the rest of his life in Larkin's doomed but unfail-
ingly dignified struggle to reconcile the golden light in the high windows

with the endlessness it comes from. His sense of inadequacy, his fear of death are in every poem. His poems could not be more personal. But, equally, they could not be more universal. Seeing the world as the hungry and thirsty see food and drink, he describes it for the benefit of those who are at home in it, their senses dulled by satiation. The reader asks: How can a man who feels like this bear to live at all?

> Life is first boredom, then fear.
> Whether or not we use it, it goes,
> And leaves what something hidden from us chose,
> And age, and then the only end of age.

But the reader gets an answer: there are duties that annul nihilism, satisfactions beyond dissatisfaction, and, above all, the miracle of continuity. Larkin's own question about what life is worth if we have to lose it he answers with the contrary question, about what life would amount to if it didn't go on without us. Awkward at the seaside, ordinary people know better in their bones than the poet among his books:

> The white steamer has gone. Like breathed-on glass
> The sunlight has turned milky. If the worst
> Of flawless weather is our falling short,
> It may be that through habit these do best,
> Coming to water clumsily undressed
> Yearly; teaching their children by a sort
> Of clowning; helping the old, too, as they ought.

Just as Larkin's resolutely prosaic organisation of a poem is its passport to the poetic, so his insight into himself is his window on the world. He is the least solipsistic of artists. Unfortunately, this fact has now become less clear. Too much light has been shed. Of the poems previously unpublished in book form, a few are among his greatest achievements, many more one would not now want to be without, and all are good to have. But all the poems he didn't publish have been put in chronological order of composition along with those he did publish, instead of being given a separate section of their own. There is plenty of editorial apparatus to tell you how the original slim volumes were made up, but the strategic economy of their initial design has been lost.

All three of the original volumes start and end with the clean, dramatic decisiveness of a curtain going up and coming down again. The cast is not loitering in the auditorium beforehand. Nor is it to be found hanging out in the car park afterward. *The Less Deceived* starts with 'Lines on a Young Lady's Photograph Album', which laments a lost love but with no confessions of the poet's personal inadequacy. It ends with 'At Grass', which is not about him but about horses: a bugle call at sunset.

> Only the groom, and the groom's boy,
> With bridles in the evening come.

Similarly, *The Whitsun Weddings* starts and ends without a mention of the author. The first poem, 'Here', is an induction into 'the surprise of a large town' that sounds as if it might be Hull. No one who sounds as if he might be Larkin puts in an appearance. Instead, other people do, whose 'removed lives/ Loneliness clarifies'. The last poem in the book, 'An Arundel Tomb', is an elegy written in a church crypt which is as sonorous as Gray's written in a churchyard, and no more petulant: that things pass is a fact made majestic, if not welcome.

As for *High Windows*, the last collection published while he was alive, it may contain, in 'The Building', his single most terror-stricken – and, indeed, terrifying – personal outcry against the intractable fact of death, but it begins and ends with the author well in the background. 'To the Sea', the opening poem, the one in which the white steamer so transfixingly gets stuck in the afternoon, is his most thoroughgoing celebration of the element that he said he would incorporate into his religion if he only had one: water. 'The Explosion' closes the book with a heroic vision of dead coal miners which could be called a hymn to immortality if it did not come from a pen that devoted so much effort to pointing out that mortality really does mean what it says.

These two poems, 'To the Sea' and 'The Explosion', which in *High Windows* are separated by the whole length of a short but weighty book, can be taken together as a case in point, because, as the chronological arrangement of the *Collected Poems* now reveals, they were written together, or almost. The first is dated October 1969, and the second is dated 5 January 1970. Between them in *High Windows* come poems dated anything from five years earlier to three years later. This is only one instance, unusually striking but typical rather than exceptional, of how Larkin moved poems around through compositional time so that they would make in emotional space the kind of sense he wanted, and not another kind. Though there were poems he left out of *The Less Deceived* and put into *The Whitsun Weddings*, it would be overbold to assume that any poem, no matter how fully achieved, that he wrote before *High Windows* but did not publish in it would have found a context later – or even earlier if he had been less cautious. Anthony Thwaite goes some way toward assuming exactly that – or, at any rate, suggesting it – when he says that Larkin had been stung by early refusals and had later on repressed excellent poems even when his friends urged him to publish them. Some of these poems, as we now see, were indeed excellent, but if a man is so careful to arrange his works in a certain order it is probably wiser to assume that when he subtracts something he is adding to the arrangement.

Toward the end of his life, in the years after *High Windows*, Larkin famously dried up. Poems came seldom. Some of those that did come equalled his best, and 'Aubade' was among his greatest. Larkin thought highly enough of it himself to send it out in pamphlet form to his friends and acquaintances, and they were quickly on the telephone to one another quoting phrases and lines from it. Soon it was stanzas, and in London there is at least one illustrious playwright who won't go home from a dinner party before he has found an excuse to recite the whole thing.*

---

* This brief anecdote is repeated later in the book and the anonymous playwright is named.

This is a special way of being afraid
No trick dispels. Religion used to try,
That vast, moth-eaten musical brocade
Created to pretend we never die,
And specious stuff that says *No rational being
Can fear a thing it will not feel*, not seeing
That this is what we fear – no sight, no sound,
No touch or taste or smell, nothing to think with,
Nothing to love or link with,
The anaesthetic from which none come round . . .

Had Larkin lived longer, there would eventually have had to be one more slim volume, even if slimmer than slim. But that any of the earlier suppressed poems would have gone into it seems very unlikely. The better they are, the better must have been his reasons for holding them back. Admittedly, the fact that he did not destroy them is some evidence that he was not averse to their being published after his death. As a seasoned campaigner for the preservation of British holograph manuscripts – he operated on the principle that papers bought by American universities were lost to civilisation – he obviously thought that his own archive should be kept safe. But the question of how the suppressed poems should be published has now been answered: some other way than this. Arguments for how good they are miss the point, because it is not their weakness that is inimical to his total effect; it is their strength. There are hemistiches as riveting as anything he ever made public.

Dead leaves desert in thousands . . .

He wrote that in 1953 and sat on it for more than thirty years. What other poet would not have got it into print somehow? The two first lines of a short poem called 'Pigeons', written in 1957, are a paradigm distillation of his characteristic urban pastoralism:

> On shallow slates the pigeons shift together,
> Backing against a thin rain from the west . . .

Even more remarkable, there were whole big poems so close to being fully realised that to call them unfinished sounds like effrontery. Not only would Larkin never let a flawed poem through for the sake of its strong phrasing; he would sideline a strong poem because of a single flaw. But 'Letter to a Friend about Girls', written in 1959, has nothing frail about it except his final indecision about whether Horatio is writing to Hamlet or Hamlet to Horatio. The writer complains that the addressee gets all the best girls without having to think about it, while he, the writer, gets, if any, only the ones he doesn't really want, and that after a long struggle.

> After comparing lives with you for years
> I see how I've been losing: all the while
> I've met a different gauge of girl from yours . . .

A brilliantly witty extended conceit, full of the scatological moral observation that Larkin and his friend Kingsley Amis jointly brought back from conversation into the literature from which it had been banished, the poem has already become incorporated into the Larkin canon that people quote to one another. So have parts of 'The Dance', which would probably have been his longest single poem if he had ever finished it. The story of an awkward, put-upon, recognisably Larkin-like lonely man failing to get together with a beautiful woman even though she seems to be welcoming his attentions, the poem could logically have been completed only by becoming a third novel to set beside *Jill* and *A Girl in Winter*. (Actually, the novel had already been written, by Kingsley Amis, and was called *Lucky Jim*.)

But there might have been a better reason for abandoning the poem. Like the Horatio poem and many of the other poems that were held back, 'The Dance' is decisive about what Larkin otherwise preferred to leave indeterminate. 'Love Again', written in 1979, at the beginning of the arid last phase in which the poems that came to

him seem more like bouts of fever than like showers of rain, states
the theme with painful clarity.

> Love again: wanking at ten past three
> (Surely he's taken her home by now?),
> The bedroom hot as a bakery . . .

What hurts, though, isn't the vocabulary. When Larkin speaks of
'Someone else feeling her breasts and cunt', he isn't speaking with
untypical bluntness: though unfalteringly well judged, his tonal range
always leaves room for foul language – shock effects are among his
favourites. The pain at this point comes from the fact that it is so
obviously Larkin talking. This time, the voice isn't coming through
a persona: it's the man himself, only at his least complex, and therefore least individual. In his oeuvre, as selected and arranged by
himself, there is a dialogue going on, a balancing of forces between
perfection of the life and of the work – a classic conflict for which
Larkin offers us a resolution second in its richness only to the later
poems of Yeats. In much of the previously suppressed poetry, the
dialogue collapses into a monologue. The man who has, at least in
part, chosen his despair, or who, at any rate, strives to convince
himself that he has, is usurped by the man who has no choice. The
second man might well be thought of as the real man, but one of
the effects of Larkin's work is to make us realise that beyond the
supposed bed-rock reality of individual happiness or unhappiness
there is a social reality of creative fulfilment, or, failing that, of public
duties faithfully carried out.

Larkin, in his unchecked personal despair, is a sacrificial goat
with the sexual outlook of a stud bull. He thinks, and sometimes
speaks, like a Robert Crumb character who has never recovered from
being beaten up by a girl in the third grade. The best guess, and the
least patronising as well, is that Larkin held these poems back because
he thought them self-indulgent – too private to be proportionate.
One of the consolations that Larkin's work offers us is that we can
be unhappy without giving in, without letting our wish to be off the

hook ('Beneath it all, desire of oblivion runs') wipe out our lives ('the million-petalled flower/ Of being here'). The ordering of the individual volumes was clearly meant to preserve this balance, which the inclusion of even a few more of the suppressed poems would have tipped.

In the *Collected Poems*, that hard-fought-for poise is quite gone. Larkin now speaks a good deal less for us all, and a good deal more for himself, than was his plain wish. That the self, the sad, dithering personal condition from which all his triumphantly assured work sprang, is now more comprehensively on view is not really a full compensation, except, perhaps, to those who aren't comfortable with an idol unless its head is made from the same clay as its feet.

On the other hand, to be given, in whatever order, all these marvellous poems that were for so long unseen is a bonus for which only a dolt would be ungrateful. Larkin's best poems are poetry better than can be said, but sayability they sumptuously offer. Larkin demands to be read aloud. His big, intricately formed stanzas, often bridging from one to the next, defeat the single breath but always invite it. As you read, the ideal human voice speaks in your head. It isn't his: as his gramophone records prove, he sounded like someone who expects to be interrupted. It isn't yours, either. It's ours. Larkin had the gift of reuniting poetry at its most artful with ordinary speech at its most unstudied – at its least literary. Though a scholar to the roots, he was not being perverse when he posed as a simple man. He thought that art should be self-sufficient. He was disturbed by the way literary studies had crowded out literature. But none of this means that he was simplistic. Though superficially a reactionary crusader against modernism, a sort of latter-day, one-man Council of Trent, he knew exactly when to leave something unexplained.

The process of explaining him will be hard to stop now that this book is available. It is still, however, a tremendous book, and, finally, despite all the candour it apparently offers, the mystery will be preserved for any reader acute enough to sense the depth under the clarity. Pushkin said that everything was on his agenda, even the disasters. Larkin knew about himself. In private hours of anguish, he commiserated with himself. But he was an artist, and that meant he was everyone; and what made him a genius was the effort and resource he brought to bear in order to meet his superior responsibility.

Larkin went to hell, but not in a handcart. From his desolation he built masterpieces, and he was increasingly disinclined to settle for anything less. About twenty years ago in Britain, it became fashionable to say that all the poetic excitement was in America. Though things look less that way now, there is no need to be just as silly in the opposite direction. The English-speaking world is a unity. Britain and the United States might have difficulty absorbing each other's poetry, but most people have difficulty with poetry anyway. In Britain, Larkin shortened the distance between the people and poetry by doing nothing for his career and everything to compose artefacts that would have an independent, memorable life apart from himself. There is no inherent reason that the American reader, or any other English-speaking reader, should not be able to appreciate the results.

Art, if it knows how to wait, wins out. Larkin had patience. For him, poetry was a life sentence. He set happiness aside to make room for it. And if it turns out that he had no control over where his misery came from, doesn't that mean that he had even more control than we thought over where it went to? Art is no less real for being artifice. The moment of truth must be prepared for. 'Nothing to love or link with,' wrote Larkin when he was fifty-five. 'Nothing to catch or claim,' he wrote when he was twenty-four, in a poem that only now sees the light. It was as if the death he feared to the end he had embraced at the start, just so as to raise the stakes.

Wolves Of Memory

HIGH WINDOWS BY PHILIP LARKIN

Larkin collections come out at the rate of one per decade: *The North Ship*, 1945; *The Less Deceived*, 1955; *The Whitsun Weddings*, 1964; *High Windows*, 1974. Not exactly a torrent of creativity: just the best. In Italy the reading public is accustomed to cooling its heels for even longer. Their top man, Eugenio Montale, has produced only five main collections, and he got started a good deal earlier. But that, in both countries, is the price one has to pay. For both the poets the parsimony is part of the fastidiousness. Neither writes an unconsidered line.

Now that the latest Larkin, *High Windows*, is finally available, it is something of a shock to find in it some poems one doesn't recognise. Clipping the poems out of magazines has failed to fill the bill – there were magazines one hadn't bargained for. As well as that, there is the surprise of finding that it all adds up even better than one had expected: the poems which one had thought of as characteristic turn out to be more than that – or rather the *character* turns out to be more than that. Larkin has never liked the idea of an artist Developing. Nor has he himself done so. But he has managed to go on clarifying what he was sent to say. The total impression of *High Windows* is of despair made beautiful. Real despair and real beauty, with not a trace of posturing in either. The book is the peer of the previous two mature collections, and if they did not exist would be just as astonishing. But they do exist (most of us could recognise any line from either one) and can't help rendering many of the themes in this third book deceptively familiar.

I think that in most of the poems here collected Larkin's ideas are being reinforced or deepened rather than repeated. But from time to time a certain predictability of form indicates that a previous discovery is being unearthed all over again. Such instances aren't difficult to spot, and it would be intemperate to betray delight at doing so. Larkin's 'forgeries' (Auden's term for self-plagiarisms) are very few. He is more original from poem to poem than almost any modern poet one can think of. His limitations, such as they are, lie deeper than that. Here again, it is not wise to be happy about spotting them. Without the limitations there would be no Larkin – the beam cuts *because* it's narrow.

It has always seemed to me a great pity that Larkin's more intelligent critics should content themselves with finding his view of life circumscribed. It is, but it is also bodied forth as art to a remarkable degree. There is a connection between the circumscription and the poetic intensity, and it's no surprise that the critics who can't see the connection can't see the separation either. They seem to think that just because the poet is (self-admittedly) emotionally wounded, the poetry is wounded too. There is always the suggestion that Larkin might handle his talent better if he were a more well-rounded character. That Larkin's gift might be part and parcel of his own peculiar nature isn't a question they have felt called upon to deal with. The whole fumbling dereliction makes you wonder if perhaps the literati in this country haven't had things a bit easy. A crash course in, say, art criticism could in most cases be recommended. Notions that Michelangelo would have painted more feminine-looking sibyls if he had not been gay, or that Toulouse-Lautrec might have been less obsessive about Jane Avril's dancing if his legs had been longer, would at least possess the merit of being self-evidently absurd. But the brain-wave about Larkin's quirky negativism, and the consequent trivialisation of his lyrical knack, is somehow able to go on sounding profound.

It ought to be obvious that Larkin is not a universal poet in the thematic sense – in fact, he is a self-proclaimed stranger to a good half, *the* good half, of life. You wonder what a critic who complains of this imagines he is praising when he allows that Larkin is still pretty good anyway, perhaps even great. What's missing in Larkin doesn't just tend to be missing, it's glaringly, achingly, unarguably missing. But the poetry is all there. The consensus about his stature is consequently encouraging, even if accomplished at the cost of a majority of its adherents misunderstanding what is really going on. At least they've got the right man.

The first poem in the book, 'To the Sea', induces a fairly heavy effect of *déjà lu*. Aren't we long used to that massive four-stanza form, that conjectural opening ('To step over the low wall . . . ') in the infinitive? Actually we aren't: he's never used them before. He's used the tone which is probably borrowed, at least in part, from Eliot's *Burnt Norton*. It's the tone that's reminiscent, and the tactics. The opening takes us back to the childhood and the lost chance of happiness, the shots that all fell wide –

> The miniature gaiety of seasides.

In the familiar way, sudden brutalities of diction bite back a remembered sweetness –

> A white steamer stuck in the afternoon . . .

Alienation is declared firmly as the memories build up –

> Strange to it now, I watch the cloudless scene:

Details well up in the mind with Proustian specificity –

> . . . and then the cheap cigars,
> The chocolate-papers, tea-leaves, and, between

> The rocks, the rusting soup-tins . . .

The mind, off guard, unmanned by recollection, lets slip the delicately expressed lyrical image –

> The white steamer has gone. Like breathed-on glass
> The sunlight has turned milky.

Whereupon, as in 'Church Going' or 'The Whitsun Weddings', the poem winds up in a sententious coda.

> . . . if the worst
> Of flawless weather is our falling short
> It may be that through habit these do best,
> Coming to water clumsily undressed
> Yearly; teaching their children by a sort
> Of clowning; helping the old, too, as they ought.

The happiness we once thought we could have can't be had, but simple people who stick to time-honoured habits probably get the best approximation of it. Larkin once said that if he were called in to construct a religion he would make use of water. Well, here it is, lapping at the knobbled feet of unquestioning plebs. Such comfort as the poem offers the reader resides in the assurance that this old habit of going to the seaside is 'still going on', even if the reader and writer no longer share it. A cold comfort, as always. Larkin tries, he has said, to preserve experience both for himself and for others, but his first responsibility is to the experience.

The next big poem is the famous three-part effort that appeared in the *Observer*, 'Livings'. A galley-proof of it is still folded into the back of my copy of *The Less Deceived*. I think it an uncanny piece of work. The proof is read to shreds, and I can still remember the day I picked it up in the office. Larkin had the idea – preserved, in concentrated form, in one of the poems in this volume, 'Posterity' – that a young American Ph.D. student called Jake Balokowsky is all set to wrap him up in an uncomprehending thesis. The first part of 'Livings' is full of stuff that Balokowsky is bound to get wrong. The minor businessman who annually books himself into 'the — Hotel in —ton for three days' speaks a vocabulary as well-rubbed and subtly anonymous as an old leather couch. Balokowsky will latch on well enough to the idea that the poem's narrator is a slave to habit,

> . . . wondering why
> I keep on coming. It's not worth it. Father's dead:
> He used to, but the business now is mine.
> It's time for change, in nineteen twenty-nine.*

What Jake will probably miss, however, is the value placed on the innocuous local newspaper, the worn decor, the ritual chat, the non-challenging pictures and the ex-Army sheets. It's dependable, it's a living, and 'living' is not a word Larkin tosses around lightly. Judging the narrator is the last thing Larkin is doing. On the contrary, he's looking for his secret. To be used to comfort is an enviable condition. Beer, whisky, cigars and silence – the privileges of the old mercantile civilisation which Larkin has been quietly celebrating most of his life, a civilisation in which a place like Leeds or Hull (see 'Friday Night in the Royal Station Hotel') counts as a capital city. There *is* another and bigger life, but Larkin doesn't underestimate this one for a minute.

In fact he conjures it up all over again in the third part of the poem. The setting this time is Oxford, probably in the late seventeenth century. The beverage is port instead of whisky, and the talk, instead of with wages, tariffs and stock, deals with advowsons, resurrections and regicide. Proofs of God's existence lie uncontested on dusty bookshelves. 'The bells discuss the hour's graduations.' Once again the feeling of indoor warmth is womb-like. Constellations sparkle over the roofs, matching the big sky draining down the estuary in Part I.

The central poem of the trio squirms like a cat caught between two cushions. Its narrator is conducting a lone love-affair with the sea:

> Rocks writhe back to sight.
> Mussels, limpets,

---

* This extract reproduces the text as it was published in the *Observer*. By the time of publication in *High Windows* in 1974, the second line had changed to 'I think it's worth while coming. Father's dead'.

> Husband their tenacity
> In the freezing slither –
> Creatures, I cherish you!

The narrator's situation is not made perfectly clear. While wanting to be just the reverse, Larkin can on occasion be a difficult poet, and here, I think, is a case of over-refinement leading to obscurity. (Elsewhere in this volume 'Sympathy in White Major' is another instance, and I have never been able to understand 'Dry Point' in *The Less Deceived*.) My guess – and a guess is not as good as an intelligent deduction – is that the speaker is a lighthouse keeper. The way the snow ('O loose moth world') swerves against the black water, and the line 'Guarded by brilliance', seem somehow to suggest that: that, or something similar. Anyway, whoever he is, the narrator is right in among the elements, watching the exploding sea and the freezing slither from seventy feet up on a stormy night. But we see at the end that he, too, is safe indoors. On the radio he hears of elsewhere. He sets out his plate and spoon, cherishing his loneliness. In this central panel of his triptych, it seems to me, Larkin is saying that the civilisations described in the side panels – one decaying, the other soon to lose its confidence – have an essence, and that this is it. The essence can be preserved in the soul of a man on his own. This is not to suggest that there is anything consolingly positive under Larkin's well-known negativism: the only consoling thing about Larkin is the quality of his art.

'High Windows', the next stand-out poem, shows an emotional progression Larkin had already made us used to.

> When I see a couple of kids
> And guess he's fucking her and she's
> Taking pills or wearing a diaphragm,
> I know this is paradise . . .

Larkin is a master of language levels and eminently qualified to use coarse language for shock effects. He never does, however. Strong language in Larkin is put in not to shock the reader but to define the narrator's personality. When Larkin's narrator in 'A Study of Reading Habits' (in *The Whitsun Weddings*) said 'Books are a load of crap' there were critics – some of them, incredibly, among his more appreciative – who allowed themselves to believe that Larkin was expressing his own opinion. (Kingsley Amis had the same kind of trouble, perhaps from the same kind of people, when he let Jim Dixon cast aspersions on Mozart.) It should be obvious at long last, however, that the diction describes the speaker. When the speaker is close to representing Larkin himself, the diction defines which Larkin it is – what mood he is in. Larkin is no hypocrite and has expressed envy of young lovers too often to go back on it here. The word 'fucking' is a conscious brutalism, a protective way of not conjuring up what's meant. However inevitable it might be that Jake Balokowsky will identify this opening sentiment as a Muggeridgean gesture of contempt, it is incumbent on us to realise that something more interesting is going on.

Everyone young is going down 'the long slide' to happiness. The narrator argues that his own elders must have thought the same about him, who was granted freedom from the fear of Hellfire in the same way that the kids are granted freedom from the fear of pregnancy. But (and here comes the clincher) attaining either freedom means no more than being lifted up to a high window, through which you see

> . . . the deep blue air, that shows
> Nothing, and is nowhere, and is endless.

There is no doubt that the narrator is calling these callous sexual activities meaningless. What's open to doubt is whether the narrator believes what he is saying, or, given that he does, whether Larkin (wheels within wheels) believes the narrator. Later in the volume there is a poem called 'Annus Mirabilis' which clearly contradicts the argument of 'High Windows'.

> Sexual intercourse began
> In nineteen sixty-three
> (Which was rather late for me) –
> Between the end of the *Chatterley* ban
> And the Beatles' first LP.

Evincing an unexpected sensitivity to tone, Jake could well detect an ironic detachment here. To help him out, there is a suggestion, in the third stanza, that the new liberty was merely licence:

> And every life became
> A brilliant breaking of the bank,
> A quite unlosable game.

It all links up with the bleak view of 'High Windows'. What Jake might not spot, however, is that it contrasts more than it compares. 'Annus Mirabilis' is a jealous poem – the fake naive rhythms are there for self-protection as much as for ironic detachment. Larkin can't help believing that sex and love ought by rights to have been easier things for his generation, and far easier for him personally. The feeling of having missed out on something is one of his preoccupations. The thing Balokowsky needs to grasp is that Larkin is not criticising modern society from a position of superiority. Over the range of his poetry, if not always in individual poems, he is very careful to allow that these pleasures might very well be thought meaningful. That he himself finds them meaningless might have something to do with himself as well as the state of the world. To the reader who has Larkin's poetry by heart, no poet seems more open. Small wonder that he finds it simply incomprehensible when critics discuss his lack of emotion. Apart from an outright yell for help, he has sent every distress signal a shy man can.

'The Old Fools' – even the ex-editor of the *Listener* blew his cool head over that one, billing it as 'marvellous' on the paper's mast-head. And marvellous it is, although very scary. There is a pronounced technical weakness in the first stanza. It is all right to rhyme 'remember' with 'September' if you make it quite clear why September can't be July. Does it mean that the Old Fools were in the Home Guard in September 1939? It's hard to know. Apart from that one point, though, the poem is utterly and distressingly explicit. Once again, the brutalism of the opening diction is a tip-off to the narrator's state of mind, which is, this time, fearful.

> What do they think has happened, the old fools,
> To make them like this? Do they somehow suppose
> It's more grown-up when your mouth hangs open and
> drools . . .

Ill-suppressed anger. The crack about supposing 'it's more grown-up' is a copybook example of Larkin's ability to compact his intelligibility without becoming ambiguous. Supposing something to be 'more grown-up' is something children do: ergo, the Old Fools are like children – one of the poem's leading themes stated in a single locution.

> Why aren't they screaming?

Leaving the reader to answer: because they don't know what's happening to them. The narrator's real fears – soon he switches to a personal 'you' – are for himself. The second stanza opens with an exultant lyrical burst: stark terror never sounded lovelier.

> At death, you break up: the bits that were you
> Start speeding away from each other for ever
> With no one to see. It's only oblivion, true:
> We had it before, but then it was going to end,
> And was all the time merging with a unique endeavour
> To bring to bloom the million-petalled flower
> Of being here.

The old, he goes on to suggest, probably live not in the here and now but 'where all happened once.' The idea takes some of its force from our awareness that that's largely where Larkin lives already – only his vision could lead to this death. The death is terrifying, but we would have to be like Larkin to share the terror completely. The reader tends to find himself shut out, glad that Larkin can speak so beautifully in his desperation but sorry that he should see the end in terms of his peculiar loneliness. There is always the edifying possibility, however, that Larkin is seeing the whole truth and the reader's defence mechanisms are working full blast.

If they are, 'The Building' will quickly break them down. Here, I think, is the volume's masterpiece – an absolute chiller, which I find myself getting by heart despite a pronounced temperamental aversion. The Building is the house of death, a Dantesque hell-hole – one thinks particularly of *Inferno* V – where people 'at that vague age that claims/ The end of choice, the last of hope' are sent to 'their appointed levels'. The ambience is standard modernist hum-drum: paperbacks, tea, rows of steel chairs like an airport lounge. You can look down into the yard and see red brick, lagged pipes, traffic. But the smell is frightening. In time everyone will find a nurse beckoning to him. The dead lie in white rows somewhere above. This, says Larkin with an undeflected power unique even for him, is what it all really adds up to. Life is a dream and we awake to this reality.

> O world,
> Your loves, your chances, are beyond the stretch
> Of any hand from here! And so, unreal,
> A touching dream to which we all are lulled
> But wake from separately. In it, conceits
> And self-protecting ignorance congeal
> To carry life . . .

There is no point in disagreeing with the man if that's the way he feels, and he wouldn't write a poem like 'The Building' if he didn't feel that way to the point of daemonic possession. He himself is well aware that there are happier ways of viewing life. It's just that he is incapable of sharing them, except for fleeting moments – and the fleeting moments do not accumulate, whereas the times in between them do. The narrator says that 'nothing contravenes/ The coming dark'. It's an inherently less interesting proposition than its opposite, and a poet forced to devote his creative effort to embodying it has only a small amount of space to work in. Nor, within the space, is he free from the paradox that his poems will become part of life, not death. From that paradox, we gain. The desperation of 'The Building' is like the desperation of Leopardi, disconsolate yet doomed to being beautiful. The advantage which accrues is one of purity – a hopeless affirmation is the only kind we really want to hear when we feel, as sooner or later everybody must, that life is a trap.

There is no certain way of separating Larkin's attitude to society from his conception of himself, but to the extent that you can, he seems to be in two minds about what the world has come to. He thinks, on the one hand, that it's probably all up; and on the other hand that youth still has a chance. On the theme of modern life being an unmitigated and steadily intensifying catastrophe he reads like his admired Betjeman in a murderous mood – no banana blush or cheery telly teeth, just a tight-browed disdain and a toxic line of invective. 'Going, Going' is particularly instructive here. In 'How Distant' we hear about

> . . . the departure of young men
> Down valleys, or watching
> The green shore past the salt-white cordage
> Rising and falling

Between the 'fraying cliffs of water' (always a good sign when there's a lot of water about) the young adventurers used to sail, in the time of what we might call genuine newness. Larkin's objections to modern innovation are centred on its lack of invention – it's all fatally predictable. Jimmy Porter was nostalgic for the future. Larkin is anticipatory about the past. He longs for the time when youth meant the possibility of a new start.

This is being young,
Assumption of the startled century

Like new store clothes,
The huge decisions printed out by feet
Inventing where they tread,
The random windows conjuring a street.

The implication being that the time of adventure is long over. But in 'Sad Steps', as the poet addresses the moon, youth is allowed some hope.

One shivers slightly, looking up there.
The hardness and the brightness and the plain
Far-reaching singleness of that wide stare

Is a reminder of the strength and pain
Of being young; that it can't come again,
But is for others undiminished somewhere.

An elegantly cadenced admission that his own view of life might be neurotic, and excellent fuel for Jake's chapter on the dialectical element in Larkin in which it is pointed out that his poems are judiciously disposed in order to illuminate one another, Yeats-style. The sun and moon, like water, bring out Larkin's expansiveness, such as it is. It's there, but you couldn't call it a bear-hug. Time is running out, as we hear in the wonderfully funny 'Vers de Société':

Only the young can be alone freely.
The time is shorter now for company,
And sitting by a lamp more often brings
Not peace, but other things.

Visions of The Building, for example.

The book ends on an up-beat. Its next to last poem, 'Show Saturday', is an extended, sumptuous evocation of country life ('Let it always be there') which has the effect of making the rural goings-on so enviably cosy that the reader feels almost as left out as the narrator. The final piece is an eerie lyric called 'The Explosion', featuring the ghosts of miners walking from the sun towards their waiting wives. It is a superb thought superbly expressed, and Larkin almost believes in it, just as in 'An Arundel Tomb' (the closing poem of *The Whitsun Weddings*) he almost believed in the survival of love. Almost believing is all right, once you've got believing out of it. But faith itself is extinct. Larkin loves and inhabits tradition as much as Betjeman does, but artistically he had already let go of it when others were only just realising it was time to cling on. Larkin is the poet of the void. The one affirmation his work offers is the possibility that when we have lost everything the problem of beauty will still remain. It's enough.

Encounter, June 1974

Smaller And Clearer

JILL AND *A GIRL IN WINTER* BY PHILIP LARKIN

Philip Larkin once told Philip Oakes – in a *Sunday Times* Magazine profile which remains, long after the demise of both the speakers, one of the essential articles on its subject – how he was going to be a novelist, until the novels stopped coming. First there was *Jill* in 1946, and then there was *A Girl in Winter* in 1947, and after those there were to be several more. But they never arrived. So Philip Larkin became the leading poet who once wrote a brace of novels, just as his friend Kingsley Amis became the leading novelist who occasionally writes poems: the creative labour was divided with the customary English decorum, providing the kind of simplified career-structures with which literary history prefers to deal.

It verges on the unmannerly to raise the point, in Larkin's case, that the novels were in no sense the work of someone who had still to find his vocation. Chronology insists that they were written at a time when his verse had not yet struck its tone – *The North Ship*, Larkin's mesmerised submission to Yeats, had only recently been published, and of *The Less Deceived*, his first mature collection, barely half the constituent poems had as yet been written. But the novels had struck their tone straight away. It is only now, by hindsight, that they seem to point forward to the poetry. Taken in their chronology, they are impressively mature and self-sufficient. If Larkin had never written a line of verse, his place as a writer would still have been secure. It would have been a smaller place than he now occupies, but still more substantial than that of, say, Denton Welch, an equivalently precocious beginner of the same period.

The self-sufficient force of Larkin's two novels is attested to by the fact that they have never quite gone away. People serious in their admiration of Larkin's poetry have usually found themselves searching out at least one of them – most commonly *Jill*, to which Larkin prefixed, in the 1964 edition, an introduction that seductively evoked the austere but ambitious Oxford of his brilliant generation and in particular was creasingly funny about Kingsley Amis. Unfortunately this preface (retained in the current paperback) implies, by its very retrospection, a status of obsolescence for the book itself. Yet the present reissue sufficiently proves that *Jill* needs no apologising for. And *A Girl in Winter* is at least as good as *Jill* and in some departments conspicuously better. Either novel is guaranteed to jolt any reader who expects Larkin to look clumsy out of his bailiwick. There are times when Larkin *does* look that, but they usually happen when he tempts himself into offering a professional rule of thumb as an aesthetic principle – a practice which can lay him open to charges of cranky insularity. None of that here. In fact quite the other thing: the novels are at ease with a range of sympathies that the later poems, even the most magnificent ones, deal with only piecemeal, although with incomparably more telling effect.

Considering that Evelyn Waugh began a comic tradition in the modern novel which only lately seems in danger of dying out, and considering Larkin's gift for sardonic comedy – a gift which by all accounts decisively influenced his contemporaries at Oxford – it is remarkable how non-comic his novels are, how completely they do not fit into the family of talents which includes Waugh and Powell and Amis. *Jill* employs many of the same properties as an Oxford novel by the young Waugh – the obscure young hero is casually destroyed by his socially superior contemporaries – but the treatment is unrelievedly sad. Larkin's hero has none of the inner strength which Amis gave Jim Dixon. Nor is there any sign of the Atkinson figures who helped Jim through the tougher parts of the maze. Young John comes up to Oxford lost and stays lost: he is not a symbol of his social condition so much as an example of how his social condition can amplify a handicap – shy ordinariness – into tragedy. All the materials of farce are present and begging to be used, but tragedy is what Larkin aims for and what he largely achieves.

The crux of the matter is John's love for Jill – a thousand dreams and one kiss. Jill is a clear forecast of the Larkin dream-girl in the poems. But if John is Larkin, he is hardly the Larkin we know to have dominated his generation at Oxford. He is someone much closer to the author's central self, the wounded personality whose deprivation has since been so clearly established in the poems. What is remarkable, however (and the same thing is remarkable about the poems, but rarely comes into question), is the way in which the hero's desolation is viewed in its entirety by the author. The author sees the whole character from without. The novel does something which very few novels by twenty-one-year-old writers have ever done. It distances autobiographical material and sets events in the global view of mature personality.

As if to prove the point, *A Girl in Winter* is a similar story of callow love, but seen from the girl's angle. The book perfectly captures the way a young woman's emotional maturity outstrips a young man's. Katherine, a young European grappling with England (an inversion of the Larkin–Amis nightmare in which the Englishman is obliged to grapple with Europe), is morally perceptive – sensitive would be the right word if it did not preclude robustness – to an unusual degree, yet Larkin is able to convince us that she is no freak. While still an adolescent she falls in love with her English pen-pal, Robin, without realising that it is Robin's sister, Jane, who is really interested in her. Time sorts out the tangle, but just when Katherine has fallen out of love Robin shows up on the off-chance of sleeping with her. Katherine quells his importunity with a few apposite remarks likely to make any male reader sweat from the palms, although finally she sleeps with him because it's less trouble than not to. Yet Katherine is allowed small comfort in her new maturity. The book is as disconsolate as its predecessor, leaving the protagonist once again facing an unsatisfactory prime.

A contributory grace in both novels, but outstanding in *A Girl in Winter*, is the sheer quality of the writing. Larkin told Oakes that he wrote the books like poems, carefully eliminating repeated words. Fastidiousness is everywhere and flamboyance non-existent: the touch is unfaltering. Katherine 'could sense his interest turning towards her, as a blind man might sense the switching on of an electric fire'. Figures of speech are invariably as quiet and effective as that. The last paragraphs of *A Girl in Winter* have something of the cadenced elegance you find at the close of *The Great Gatsby*.

Why, if Larkin could write novels like these, did he stop? To hindsight the answer is easy: because he was about to become the finest poet of his generation, instead of just one of its best novelists. A more enquiring appraisal suggests that although his aesthetic effect was rich, his stock of events was thin. In a fictional texture featuring a sore tooth and a fleeting kiss as important strands, Zen diaphanousness always threatened. (What is the sound of *one* flower being arranged?) The master lyric poet, given time, will eventually reject the idea of writing any line not meant to be remembered. Larkin, while being to no extent a dandy, is nevertheless an exquisite. It is often the way with exquisites that they graduate from full-scale prentice constructions to small-scale works of entirely original intensity, having found a large expanse limiting. Chopin is not too far-fetched a parallel. Larkin's two novels are like Chopin's two concertos: good enough to promise not merely more of the same but a hitherto unheard-of distillation of their own lyrical essence.

New Statesman, 21 March 1975

Yeats V. Hardy In Davie's Larkin

THOMAS HARDY AND BRITISH POETRY by DONALD DAVIE

In recent months Philip Larkin, based as always in Hull, and Donald Davie, back in Europe from California, have been conducting a restrained slugging-match concerning Larkin's fidelity to the *locus classicus* in modern times, as defined – or distorted, if you are of Professor Davie's persuasion – in *The Oxford Book of Twentieth-Century English Verse*. Important issues have been raised, and it will be some time before any keeper of the peace will be able to still them. The time is propitious for an assessment of Professor Davie's *Thomas Hardy and British Poetry*, which in a normal climate might be politely – and erroneously – half-praised as a well-bred squib, but for the duration of hostilities demands to be regarded as live, heavy-calibre ammunition.

Professor Davie is a poet of importance – of such importance, indeed, that his academic title can safely be set aside for the remainder of this article – and from poets of importance we want works of criticism that are less safe than strange. There is nothing safe about this volume, and a lot that is strange. *Thomas Hardy and British Poetry* is a surprisingly odd book, but it is also a considerable one. In fact, the forces ranged against each other in the current squabble can now be said to be more evenly matched than might at first appear.

A good part of the secret of what Larkin really thinks about art is distributed through the pages of *All What Jazz*, and if you want to take the weight of Larkin's aesthetic intelligence, it is to that collection (and not so much to his so-far uncollected criticisms of poetry in the magazine *Listen*, although they count) that you must go. On the Davie side, we are given, in this new book, a view of his thought which is at the very least as luminous as the one made available in *Ezra Pound: Poet as Sculptor*. When Davie talks about

Hardy he sounds like Larkin talking about jazz. To put it crudely, on their pet subjects they both talk turkey. But this doesn't mean that either man makes himself plain. Larkin worships Bix Beiderbecke and deplores Charlie Parker, believing that Parker destroyed with arid intellectualism the art to which Beiderbecke contributed by lyrical instinct. Conveying this distinction, Larkin apparently makes himself clear; but it would be a recklessly foolish critic who thought that such a distinction could be used unexamined as a light on Larkin's poetry. In poetry, Larkin is Beiderbecke and Parker combined: his criticism chooses sides among elements which are in balance within his complex creative personality. Similarly with Davie: his critical position calls for an even more cautious probing, since he is less aware of self-contradictions by the exact measure that he is more receptive to literary influence. *Thomas Hardy and British Poetry* raises confusion to the level of criticism: it is a testament to Britain's continuing fertility as an intellectual acreage in which ideas will flourish at rigour's expense, the insights blooming like orchids while the valid syllogisms wither on the vine.

Davie starts by proposing Hardy as a more important influence than Yeats on the poetry of this century. The distinction between is and ought is not firmly made, with the result that we spend a lot of our time wondering whether Hardy has been the big influence all along, or merely should have been. 'But for any poet who finds himself in the position of choosing between the two masters', Davie says, 'the choice cannot be fudged; there is no room for compromise.' The reason why there is no room for compromise is not made as clear as the ordinary reader might require. 'Hardy', it is said, 'has the effect of locking any poet whom he influences into the world of historical contingency, a world of specific places at specific times.' Yeats, apparently, doesn't have this effect: he transcends the linear unrolling of recorded time and attains, or attempts to attain, the visionary. Davie says that the reader can delight in both these approaches, but that the writer has to choose. It is difficult, at first, to see why the writer can't employ the same combinative capacity as the reader. Difficult at first, and just as difficult later.

The other important thing happening at the beginning of the book concerns Larkin. Davie mentions Larkin's conversion from Yeats to Hardy after *The North Ship* in 1946, thus tacitly proposing from the start that Larkin was doing the kind of severe choosing which Davie asserts is essential. Neither at this initial point, nor later on when Larkin is considered at length, is the possibility allowed that Yeats's influence might have lingered on alongside, or even been compounded with, Hardy's influence. One realises with unease that Davie has not only enjoyed the preface to the reissue of *The North Ship*, he has been utterly convinced by it: instead of taking Larkin's autobiographical scraps as parables, he is treating them as the realities of intellectual development. Larkin conjures up a young mind in which Hardy drives out Yeats, and Davie believes in it.

But Davie's main comments about Larkin are postponed until some sturdy ground-work has been put in on Hardy. We are told that Hardy's technique is really engineering, and that he is paying a formal tribute to Victorian technology by echoing its precisioned virtuosity. A little later on we find that Davie doesn't wholly approve of this virtuosity, and is pleased when the unwavering succession of intricately formed, brilliantly matched stanzas is allowed to break down – as in 'The Voice', where, we are assured, it breaks down under pressure of feeling.

A crucial general point about technique has bulkily arisen, but Davie miraculously succeeds in failing to notice it. At one stage he is almost leaning against it, when he says that Hardy was usually 'highly skilled indeed but disablingly modest', or even 'very ambitious technically, and unambitious every other way.' For some reason it doesn't occur to Davie that having made these admissions he is bound to qualify his definition of technique in poetry. But not only does he not qualify it – he ups the stakes. Contesting Yeats's insistence that Hardy lacked technical accomplishment, Davie says that 'In sheer *accomplishment*, especially of prosody, Hardy beats Yeats hands down' (his italics). Well, it's a poser. Yeats's critical remark about Hardy doesn't matter much more than any other of Yeats's critical remarks about anybody, but Davie's rebuttal of it matters centrally to his own argument. He is very keen to set Yeats and Hardy off against each other: an opposition which will come in handy when he gets to Larkin. But keenness must have been bordering on fervour when he decided that Hardy had Yeats beaten technically in every department except something called 'craft' – which last attribute, one can be forgiven for thinking, ought logically to take over immediately as the main subject of the book.

Davie argues convincingly that we need to see below the intricate surface form of Hardy's poems to the organic forms beneath. But he is marvellously reluctant to take his mind off the technical aspects of the surface form and get started on the problem of what technical aspects the organic form might reasonably be said to have. 'We must learn to look through apparent symmetry to the real asymmetry beneath.' We certainly must, and with Hardy, Davie has. But what Davie has not learnt to see is that with Yeats the symmetry and asymmetry are the same thing – that there is no distance between the surface form and the organic form, the thing being both all art and all virtuosity at the same time. Why, we must wonder, is Davie so reluctant to see Yeats as the formal master beside whom Hardy is simply an unusually interesting craftsman? But really that is a rephrasing of the same question everybody has been asking for years: the one about what Davie actually means when he praises Ezra Pound as a prodigious technician. Is it written in the stars that Donald Davie, clever in so many other matters, will go on to his grave being obtuse in this? Why can't he see that the large, argued Yeatsian strophe is a technical achievement thoroughly dwarfing not only Pound's imagism, but also Hardy's tricky stanzas?

Davie is continually on the verge of finding Hardy deficient as a working artist, but circumvents the problem by calling him a marvellous workman whose work tended to come out wrong for other reasons. In 'During Wind and Rain' he detects a 'wonderfully fine ear', which turns out to be a better thing than 'expertise in prosody' – the wonderfully fine ear being 'a human skill' and not just a 'technical virtuosity'. It ought to follow that knowing how to get the ear working while keeping the virtuosity suppressed is of decisive importance to poetic technique. It ought to follow further that because Hardy couldn't do this – he spent a lot of his time being at odds with himself as a poet. What Davie is struggling to say is that Hardy wasn't enough of an artist to make the best of the art that was in him. But the quickness of the pen deceives the brain, and Davie manages to say everything but that.

The strictures Davie *does* put on Hardy are harsh but inscrutable. There is in Hardy a 'crucial selling-short of the poetic vocation'. In the last analysis, we learn, Hardy, unlike Pound and Pasternak (and here Yeats, Hopkins and Eliot also get a mention), doesn't give us a transformed reality – doesn't give us entry 'into a world that is truer and more real than the world we know from statistics or scientific induction or common sense'. This stricture is inscrutable for two main reasons. First, Hardy spent a lot of his time establishing a version of reality in which, for example, lovers could go on being spiritually joined together after death: nothing scientific about that. Second, even if he had not been at pains to establish such a version of reality – even if his themes had been resolutely mundane – his poetry, if successful, would have done it for him. In saying that Hardy's poetry doesn't transform statistical, scientific reality, Davie is saying that Hardy hasn't written poetry at all.

It should be obvious that Davie, while trying to praise Hardy as an artist, is actually diminishing him in that very department. Less obviously, he is also diminishing art. To look for a life-transforming theme, surely, is as self-defeating as to look for a life-enhancing one. Good poetry transforms and enhances life *whatever it says*. That is one of the reasons why we find it so special. In this case, as in so many others, one regrets the absence in English literary history of a thoroughly nihilistic poet. The Italians had Leopardi, who in hating existence could scarcely be said to have been kidding. Faced with his example, they were obliged at an early date to realise that there is poetry which can deny a purpose to life and yet still add to its point.

Larkin, Davie insists, follows Hardy and not Yeats. 'Larkin has testified to that effect repeatedly', he announces, clinching the matter.

Yeats's influence was 'a youthful infatuation'. The ground is well laid for a thorough-going misunderstanding of Larkin on every level, and after a few back-handed compliments ('The narrowness of range . . . might seem to suggest that he cannot bear the weight of significance that I want to put on him, as the central figure in English poetry over the past twenty years' – narrowness of range as compared with whom? With people who write worse?) Davie buckles down to the task.

Hardy, we have already learnt, was neutral about industrialism because his technique mirrored it: his skill as a constructor implicated him. With Larkin it is otherwise. Larkin can feel free to hate industrialism because he has no special sense of himself as a technician: 'The stanzaic and metrical symmetries which he mostly aims at are achieved skilfully enough, but with none of that bristling expertise of Hardy which sets itself, and surmounts, intricate technical challenge.'

By this stage of the book it is no longer surprising, just saddening, that Davie can't draw the appropriate inferences from his own choice of words. Being able to quell the bristle and find challenges other than the kind one sets oneself – isn't that the true skill? The awkward fact is that unless we talk about diction, and get down to the elementary stylistic analysis which would show how Larkin borrowed Hardy's use of, say, hyphenated compounds, then it is pretty nearly impossible to trace Larkin's technical debt to Hardy. Not that Davie really tries. But apart from understandably not trying that, Davie clamorously doesn't try to find out about Larkin's technical debt to Yeats. And the inspiration for the big, matched stanzas of 'The Whitsun Weddings' is not in Hardy's 'intricacy' but in the rhetorical majesty of Yeats. In neglecting to deal with that inspiration, Davie limits his meaning of the word 'technique' to something critically inapplicable. Technically, Larkin's heritage is a combination of Hardy and Yeats – it can't possibly be a substitution of the first by the second. The texture of Larkin's verse is all against any such notion.

Mistaking Larkin's way of working is a mere prelude to mistaking his manner of speaking, and some thunderous misreadings follow as a consequence. In Larkin, we are told, 'there is to be no historical perspective, no measuring of present against past'. Applied to the author of 'An Arundel Tomb', this assertion reminds us of the old Stephen Potter ploy in which a reviewer selected the characteristic for which an author was most famous and then attacked him for not having enough of it.

According to Davie, Larkin is a Hardyesque poet mainly in the sense that he, too, 'may have sold poetry short'. With Larkin established as such a baleful influence, the problem becomes how to 'break out of the greyly constricting world of Larkin'. Davie enlists the poetry of Charles Tomlinson to help us do this, but it might have been more useful to linger awhile and ask if Larkin isn't already doing a good deal by himself to help us get clear of his dreary mire – by going on writing, that is, with the kind of intensity which lit up the gloom and made us notice him in the first place. Here again, and ruinously, Davie is dealing in every reality except the realities of art. He cannot or will not see that Larkin's grimness of spirit is not by itself the issue. The issue concerns the gratitude we feel for such a grimness of spirit producing such a beauty of utterance.

Near the end of the book, Davie draws a useful distinction between poets and prophets. The prophet is above being fair-minded: the poet is not. The poet helps to shape culture, with which the prophet is at war. Prophetic poetry is necessarily an inferior poetry.

To this last point one can think of exceptions, but generally this is well said, and leaves the reader wondering why Davie did not then go back and find something centrally and vitally praiseworthy in the limitations of the Hardy tradition. Because it is the Hardy tradition which says that you can't be entirely confident of knowing everything that reality contains, let alone of transcending it. The Hardy tradition is one of a mortal scale. It does *not* hail the super-human. As Larkin might put it, it isn't in the exaltation business. That is the real point which Davie has worriedly been half-making all along. In a striking way, *Thomas Hardy and British Poetry* is an eleventh-hour rejection of Davie's early gods. Somewhere in there among the dust and hubbub there is a roar of suction indicating that the air might soon be cleared.

The North Window

To stay, as Mr Larkin stays, back late
Checking accessions in the Brynmor Jones
Library (the clapped date-stamp, punch-drunk, rattling,
The sea-green tinted windows turning slate,
The so-called Reading Room deserted) seems
A picnic at first blush. No Rolling Stones
Manqués or Pink Floyd simulacra battling
Their way to low-slung pass-marks head in hands:
Instead, unpeopled silence. Which demands

Reverence, and calls nightly like bad dreams
To make sure that that happens. Here he keeps
Elected frith, his thanedom undespited,
Ensconced against the mating-mandrill screams
Of this week's Students' Union Gang-Bang Sit-in,
As wet winds scour the Wolds. The Moon-cold deeps
Are cod-thronged for the trawlers now benighted,
Far North. The inland cousin to the sail-maker
Can still bestride the boundaries of the way-acre,

The barley-ground and furzle-field unwritten
Fee simple failed to guard from Marks and Spencer's
Stock depot some time back. (Ten years, was it?)
Gull, lapwing, redshank, oyster-catcher, bittern
(Yet further out: shearwater, fulmar, gannet)
Police his mud-and-cloud-ashlared defences.

Intangible revetments! On deposit,
Chalk thick below prevents the Humber seeping
Upward to where he could be sitting sleeping,

So motionless he lowers. Screwed, the planet
Swivels towards its distant, death-dark pocket
He opens out his notebook at a would-be
Poem, ashamed by now that he began it.
Grave-skinned with grief, such Hardy-hyphened diction,
Tight-crammed as pack ice, grates. What keys unlock it?
It's all gone wrong. Fame isn't as it should be –
No, nothing like. 'The town's not been the same,'
He's heard slags whine, 'since Mr Larkin came.'

Sir John arriving with those science-fiction
Broadcasting pricks and bitches didn't help.
And those Jap PhDs, their questionnaires!
(Replying 'Sod off, Slant-Eyes' led to friction.)
He conjures envied livings less like dying:
Sharp cat-house stomp and tart-toned, gate-mouthed yelp
Of Satchmo surge undulled, dispersing cares
Thought reconvenes. In that way She would kiss,
The Wanted One. But other lives than this –

Fantastic. Pages spread their blankness. Sighing.
He knuckles down to force-feed epithets.
Would Love have eased the joints of his iambs?
He can't guess, and by now it's no use trying.
A sweet ache spreads from cramp-gripped pen to limb:
The stanza next to last coheres and sets.
As rhyme and rhythm, tame tonight like lambs,
Entice him to the standard whirlwind finish,
The only cry no distances diminish

Comes hurtling soundless from Creation's rim
Earthward – the harsh *recitativo secco*
Of spaces between stars. He hears it sing.
That voice of utmost emptiness. To him.
Declaring he has always moved too late,
And hinting, its each long-lost blaze's echo
Lack-lustre as a Hell-bent angel's wing,
That what – as if he needed telling twice –
Comes next makes this lot look like Paradise.

TLS, 26 July 1974

On Larkin's Wit

There is no phrase in Philip Larkin's poetry which has not been turned, but then any poet tries to avoid flat writing, even at the cost of producing overwrought banality. Larkin's dedication to compressed resonance is best studied, in the first instance, through his prose. The prefaces to the reissues of *Jill* and *The North Ship* are full of sentences that make you smile at their neat richness even when they are not meant to be jokes, and that when they are meant to be jokes – as in the evocation of the young Kingsley Amis at Oxford in the preface to *Jill* – make you wish that the article went on as long as the book. But there is a whole book which does just that: *All What Jazz*, the collection of Larkin's *Daily Telegraph* jazz record review columns, which was published in 1970. Having brought the book out, Faber seemed nervous about what to do with it next. I bought two copies marked down to 75p each in a Cardiff newsagent's and wish now that I had bought ten. I thought at the time that *All What Jazz* was the best available expression by the author himself of what he believed art to be. I still think so, and would contend in addition that no wittier book of criticism has ever been written.

To be witty does not necessarily mean to crack wise. In fact it usually means the opposite: wits rarely tell jokes. Larkin's prose flatters the reader by giving him as much as he can take in at one time. The delight caused has to do with collusion. Writer and reader are in cahoots. Larkin has the knack of donning cap and bells while still keeping his dignity. For years he feigned desperation before the task of conveying the real desperation induced in him by the saxophone playing of John Coltrane. The metaphors can be pursued through the book – they constitute by themselves a kind of extended solo, of which the summary sentence in the book's introductory essay should be regarded as the coda. 'With John Coltrane metallic and passionless nullity gave way to exercises in gigantic absurdity, great boring excursions on not-especially-attractive themes during which all possible changes were rung, extended investigations of oriental tedium, long-winded and portentous demonstrations of religiosity.' This final grandiose flourish was uttered in 1968.

But the opening note was blown in 1961, when Larkin, while yet prepared (cravenly, by his own later insistence) to praise Coltrane as a hard-thinking experimenter, referred to 'the vinegary drizzle of his tone'. In 1962 he was still in two minds, but you could already guess which mind was winning. 'Coltrane's records are, paradoxically, nearly always both interesting and boring, and I certainly find myself listening to them in preference to many a less adventurous set.' Notable at this stage is that he did not risk a metaphor, in which the truth would have more saliently protruded. In May 1963 there is only one mind left talking. To the eighth track of a Thelonious Monk album, 'John Coltrane contributes a solo of characteristic dreariness.'

By December of that same year Larkin's line on this topic has not only lost all its qualifications but acquired metaphorical force. Coltrane is referred to as 'the master of the thinly disagreeable' who 'sounds as if he is playing for an audience of cobras'. This squares up well with the critic's known disgust that the joyous voicing of the old jazz should have so completely given way to 'the cobra-coaxing cacophonies of Calcutta'. In 1965 Larkin was gratified to discover that his opinion of Coltrane's achievement was shared by the great blues-shouter Jimmy Rushing. 'I don't think he can play his instrument,' said Rushing. 'This,' Larkin observed, 'accords very well with my own opinion that Coltrane sounds like nothing so much as a club bore who has been metamorphosed by a fellow-member of magical powers into a pair of bagpipes.' (Note Larkin's comic timing, incidentally: a less witty writer would have put 'metamorphosed into a pair of bagpipes by a fellow-member of magical powers', and so halved the effect.) Later in the same piece he expanded the attack into one of those generally pertinent critical disquisitions in which

All What Jazz is so wealthy. 'His solos seem to me to bear the same relation to proper jazz solos as those drawings of running dogs, showing their legs in all positions so that they appear to have about fifty of them, have to real drawings. Once, they are amusing and even instructive. But the whole point of drawing is to choose the right line, not drawing fifty alternatives. Again, Coltrane's choice and treatment of themes is hypnotic, repetitive, monotonous: he will rock backwards and forwards between two chords for five minutes, or pull a tune to pieces like someone subtracting petals from a flower.' Later in the piece there is an atavistic gesture towards giving the Devil his due, but by the vividness of his chosen figures of speech the critic has already shown what he really thinks.

'I can thoroughly endorse', wrote Larkin in July 1966, 'the sleeve of John Coltrane's *Ascension* (HMV), which says "This record cannot be loved or understood in one sitting." ' In November of the same year he greeted Coltrane's religious suite 'Meditations' as 'the most astounding piece of ugliness I have ever heard'. After Coltrane's death in 1977 Larkin summed up the departed hero's career. '. . . I do not remember ever suggesting that his music was anything but a pain between the ears . . . Was I wrong?' In fact, as we have seen, Larkin had once allowed himself to suggest that the noises Coltrane made might at least be interesting, but by now tentativeness had long given way to a kind of fury, as of someone defending a principle against his own past weakness. 'That reedy, catarrhal tone . . . that insolent egotism, leading to 45-minute versions of "My Favourite Things" until, at any rate in Britain, the audience walked out, no doubt wondering why they had ever walked in . . . pretension as a way of life . . . wilful and hideous distortion of tone that offered squeals, squeaks, Bronx cheers and throttled slate-pencil noises for serious consideration . . . dervish-like heights of hysteria.' It should be remembered, if this sounds like a grave being danced on, that Larkin's was virtually the sole dissenting critical voice. Coltrane died in triumph and Larkin had every right to think at the time that to express any doubts about the stature of the deceased genius was to whistle against the wind.

The whole of *All What Jazz* is a losing battle. Larkin is arguing in support of entertainment at a time when entertainment was steadily yielding ground to portentous significance. His raillery against the saxophonists is merely the most strident expression of a general argument which he goes on elaborating as its truth becomes more clear to himself. In a quieter way he became progressively disillusioned with Miles Davis. In January 1962 it was allowed that in an informal atmosphere Davis could produce music 'very far from the egg-walking hushedness' he was given to in the studio. In October of the same year Larkin gave him points for bonhomie. 'According to the sleeve, Davis actually smiled twice at the audience during the evening and there is indeed a warmth about the entire proceedings that makes this a most enjoyable LP.' But by the time of *Seven Steps to Heaven* a year later, Davis has either lost what little attraction he had or else Larkin has acquired the courage of his convictions: '. . . his lifeless muted tone, at once hollow and unresonant, creeps along only just in tempo, the ends of the notes hanging down like Dali watches . . .' In 1964, Larkin begged to dissent from the enthusiastic applause recorded on the live album *Miles Davis in Europe*: '. . . the fact that he can spend seven or eight minutes playing "Autumn Leaves" without my recognising or liking the tune confirms my view of him as a master of rebarbative boredom.' A year later he was reaching for the metaphors. 'I freely confess that there have been times recently, when almost anything – the shape of a patch on the ceiling, a recipe for rhubarb jam read upside down in the paper – has seemed to me more interesting than the passionless creep of a Miles Davis trumpet solo.' But in this case the opening blast was followed by a climb-down. 'Davis is his usual bleak self, his notes wilting at the edges as if with frost, spiky at up-tempos, and while he is still not my ideal of comfortable listening his talent is clearly undiminished.' This has the cracked chime of a compromise. The notes, though wilting as if with frost instead of like Dali watches, are nevertheless still wilting, and it is clear from the whole drift of Larkin's criticism that he places no value on uncomfortable listening as such. A 1966 review sounds more straightforward: '. . . for me it was an experience in pure duration. Some of it must have been quite hard to do.'

But in Larkin's prose the invective which implies values is always matched by the encomium which states them plainly. He jokes less when praising than when attacking but the attention he pays to evocation is even more concentrated. The poem 'For Sidney Bechet', where his voice falls like an enormous yes, can be matched for unforced reverence in the critical prose: '. . . the marvellous "Blue Horizon", six choruses of slow blues in which Bechet climbs without interruption or hurry from lower to upper register, his clarinet tone at first thick and throbbing, then soaring like Melba in an extraordinary blend of lyricism and power that constituted the unique Bechet voice, commanding attention the instant it sounded.' He is similarly eloquent about the 'fire and shimmer' of Bix Beiderbecke and of the similes he attaches to Pee Wee Russell there is no end – Russell's clarinet seems to function in Larkin's imagination as a kind of magic flute. He thought the same about Billie Holiday's voice, although he was under no illusion about the dangers that she faced: in the world into which she was born, she was always fighting fate.

'. . . here is the buoyant Billie of "This Year's Kisses", "Did I Remember?" and "A Fine Romance". Here, too, is a bouquet of solos from some of the best players of an era that had achieved sophistication and taste without losing drive and simplicity, best exemplified perhaps not by the bland, allusive tenor of Lester Young but Teddy Wilson's crisp, single-fingered piano that was in itself an innovation.'

The emphasis, in Larkin's admiration for all these artists, is on their ground-breaking creativity. What they do would not have its infinite implications if it did not spring from fundamental emotion which we all share. It can be argued that Larkin is needlessly dismissive of Duke Ellington and Charlie Parker. There is plenty of evidence to warrant including him in the school of thought known among modern jazz buffs as 'mouldy fig'. But there is nothing retrograde about the aesthetic underlying his irascibility. The same aesthetic underlies his literary criticism and everything else he writes. Especially it underlies his poetry. Indeed it is not even an aesthetic: it is a world view, of the kind which invariably forms the basis of any great artistic personality. Modernism, according to Larkin, 'helps us neither to enjoy nor endure'. He defines modernism as intellectualised art. Against intellectualism he proposes, not anti-intellectualism – which would be just another coldly willed programme – but trust in the validity of emotion. What the true artist says from instinct, the true critic will hear by the same instinct. There may be more than instinct involved, but nothing real will be involved without it.

> The danger, therefore, of assuming that everything played today in jazz has a seed of solid worth stems from the fact that so much of it is tentative, experimental, private . . . And for this reason one has to fall back on the old dictum that a critic is only as good as his ear. His ear will tell him instantly whether a piece of music is vital, musical, exciting, or cerebral, mock-academic, dead, long before he can read Don DeMichael on the subject, or learn that it is written in inverted nineteenths, or in the Stygian mode, or recorded at the NAACP Festival at Little Rock. He must hold on to the principle that the only reason for praising a work is that it pleases, and the way to develop his critical sense is to be more acutely aware of whether he is being pleased or not.

What Larkin might have said on his own behalf is that critical prose can be subjected to the same test. His own criticism appeals so directly to the ear that he puts himself in danger of being thought trivial, especially by the mock academic. Like Amis's, Larkin's readability seems so effortless that it tends to be thought of as something separate from his intelligence. But readability *is* intelligence. The vividness of Larkin's critical style is not just a token of his seriousness but the embodiment of it. His wit is there not only in the cutting jokes but in the steady work of registering his interest. It is easy to see that he is being witty when he says that Miles Davis and Ornette Coleman stand in evolutionary relationship to each other 'like green apples and stomach ache'. But he is being equally witty when he mentions

Ruby Braff's 'peach-fed' cornet. A critic's language is not incidental to him: its intensity is a sure measure of his engagement and a persuasive hint at the importance of what he is engaged with.

A critical engagement with music is one of the several happy coincidences which unite Larkin's career with Montale's. If Larkin's *Listen* articles on poetry were to be reprinted the field of comparison would be even more instructive, since there are good reasons for thinking that these two poets come up with remarkably similar conclusions when thinking about the art they practise. On music they often sound like the same man talking. Montale began his artistic career as a trained opera singer and his main area of musical criticism has always been classical music, but he writes about it the same way Larkin writes about jazz, with unfaltering intelligibility, a complete trust in his own ear, and a deep suspicion of any work which draws inspiration from its own technique. In Italy his collected music criticism is an eagerly awaited book, but then in Italy nobody is surprised that a great poet should have written a critical column for so many years of his life. Every educated Italian knows that Montale's music notices are all of a piece with the marvellous body of literary criticism collected in *Auto da fé* and *Sulla poesia*, and that his whole critical corpus is the natural complement to his poetry. In Britain the same connection is harder to make, even though Larkin has deservedly attained a comparable position as a national poet. In Britain the simultaneous pursuit of poetry and regular critical journalism is regarded as versatility at best. The essential unity of Larkin's various activities is not much remarked.

But if we do not remark it we miss half of his secret. While maintaining an exalted idea of the art he practises, Larkin never thinks of it as an inherently separate activity from the affairs of everyday. He has no special poetic voice. What he brings out is the poetry that is already in the world. He has cherished the purity of his own first responses. Like all great artists he has never lost touch with the child in his own nature. The language of even the most intricately wrought Larkin poem is already present in recognisable embryo when he describes the first jazz musicians ever to capture his devotion. 'It was the drummer I concentrated on, sitting as he did on a raised platform behind a battery of cowbells, temple blocks, cymbals, tomtoms and (usually) a Chinese gong, his drums picked out in flashing crimson or ultramarine brilliants.' There are good grounds for calling Larkin a pessimist, but it should never be forgotten that the most depressing details in the poetry are seen with the same eye that loved those drums. The proof is in the unstinting vitality of language.

As in the criticism, so in the poetry, wit can be divided usefully into two kinds, humorous and plain. There is not much need to rehearse the first kind. Most of us have scores of Larkin's lines, hemistiches and phrases in our heads, to make us smile whenever we think of them, which is as often as the day changes. I can remember the day in 1962 when I first opened *The Less Deceived* and was snared by a line in the first poem, 'Lines on a Young Lady's Photograph Album'. 'Not quite your class, I'd say, dear, on the whole.' What a perfectly timed pentameter! How subtly and yet how unmistakably it defined the jealousy of the speaker! Who on earth was Philip Larkin? Dozens of subsequent lines in the same volume made it clearer: he was a supreme master of language levels, snapping into and out of a tone of voice as fast as it could be done without losing the reader. Bringing the reader in on it – the deep secret of popular seriousness. Larkin brought the reader in on it even at the level of prosodic technique.

Flagged, and the figurehead with golden tits
Arching our way, it never anchors; it's . . .

He got you smiling at a rhyme. 'Church Going' had the ruin-bibber, randy for antique, 'Toads' had the pun on Shakespeare, 'Stuff your pension!' being the stuff dreams are made on. You couldn't get halfway through the book without questioning, and in many cases revising, your long-nursed notions about poetic language. Here was a disciplined yet unlimited variety of tone, a scrupulosity that could contain anything, an all-inclusive decorum.

In *The Whitsun Weddings*, 'Mr Bleaney' has the Bodies and 'Naturally the Foundation will Bear Your Expenses' has the ineffable Mr Lal. 'Sunny Prestatyn' features Titch Thomas and in 'Wild Oats' a girl painfully reminiscent of Margaret in *Lucky Jim* is finally shaken loose 'after about five rehearsals'. In 'Send No Money' 'the trite untransferable/ Truss-advertisement, truth' takes you back to the cobra-coaxing cacophonies of Calcutta, not to mention forward to Amis's nitwit not fit to shift shit. Even *High Windows*, the bleakest of Larkin's slim volumes, has things to make you laugh aloud. In 'The Card-Players' Jan van Hogspeuw and Old Prijck perhaps verge on the coarse but Jake Balokowsky, the hero of 'Posterity', has already entered the gallery of timeless academic portraits, along with Professor Welch and the History Man. 'Vers de Société' has 'the bitch/ Who's read nothing but *Which*'. In Larkin's three major volumes of poetry the jokes on their own would be enough to tell you that wit is alive and working.

But it is working far more pervasively than that. Larkin's poetry is all witty – which is to say that there is none of his language which does not confidently rely on the intelligent reader's capacity to apprehend its play of tone. On top of the scores of fragments that make us laugh, there are the hundreds which we constantly recall with a welcome sense of communion, as if our own best thoughts had been given their most concise possible expression. If Auden was right about the test of successful writing being how often the reader thinks of it, Larkin passed it long ago. To quote even the best examples would be to fill half this book, but perhaps it will bear saying again, this time in the context of his poetry, that between Larkin's humorous wit and his plain wit there is no discontinuity. Only the man who invented the golden tits could evoke the black-sailed unfamiliar. To be able to make fun of the randy ruin-bibber is the necessary qualification for writing the magnificent last stanza of 'Church Going'. You need to have been playfully alliterative with the trite untransferable truss-advertisement before you can be lyrically alliterative with the supine stationary voyage of the dead lovers in 'An Arundel Tomb'. There is a level of seriousness which only those capable of humour can reach.

Similarly there is a level of maturity which only those capable of childishness can reach. The lucent comb of 'The Building' can be seen by us only because it has been so intensely seen by Larkin, and it has been so intensely seen by him only because his eyes, behind those thick glasses, retain the naive curiosity which alone makes the adult gaze truly penetrating. Larkin's poetry draws a bitterly sad picture of modern life but it is full of saving graces, and they are invariably as disarmingly recorded as in a child's diary. The paddling at the seaside, the steamer in the afternoon, the ponies at Show Saturday – they are all done with crayons and coloured pencils. He did not put away childish things and it made him more of a man. It did the same for Montale: those who have ever read about the amulet in 'Dora Markus' or the children with tin swords in 'Caffè a Rapallo' are unlikely to forget them when they read Larkin; a third name could be added: Mandelstam. When Mandelstam forecast his own death he willed that his spirit should be resurrected in the form of children's games. All three poets represent, for their respective countrymen, the distilled lyricism of common speech. With all three poets the formal element is highly developed – in the cases of Larkin and Mandelstam to the uppermost limit possible – and yet none of them fails to reassure his readers, even during the most intricately extended flight of verbal music, that the tongue they speak is the essential material of his rhythmic and melodic resource.

In Philip Larkin's non-poetic poetic language, the language of extremely well-written prose, despair is expressed through beauty and becomes beautiful too. His argument is with himself and he is bound to lose. He can call up death more powerfully than almost any other poet ever has, but he does so in the commanding voice of life. His linguistic exuberance is the heart of him. Joseph Brodsky, writing about Mandelstam, called lyricism the ethics of language.

Larkin's wit is the ethics of his poetry. It brings his distress under our control. It makes his personal unhappiness our universal exultation. Armed with his wit, he faces the worst on our behalf, and brings it to order. A romantic sensibility classically disciplined, he is, in the only sense of the word likely to last, modern after all. By rebuilding the ruined bridge between poetry and the general reading public he has given his art a future, and you can't get more modern than that.

Published in *Larkin at Sixty*, edited by
Anthony Thwaite (Faber, London), 1982

Librarian: P. A. Larkin, C.B.E., C.Lit., M.A., D.Lit., D.Litt., F.R.S.L., F.L.A.

4th May, 1982.

Clive James, Esq.,
Jonathan Cape Ltd.,
30 Bedford Square,
LONDON.
WC1B 3EL

Dear Clive,

How extremely kind of you to send me a copy of From the Land of Shadows!
In fact I had already bought it, having found a copy in the brilliant little local book-
shop (which, needless to say, is closing down in July), but I can flog that copy to
the Library. Rank has its privileges, as the Captain said when asked to explain
the presence of 74 empty whisky bottles in his cabin.

I much enjoyed reading the pieces about authors I knew (how I agree about
The Honourable Schoolboy!), and now am gingerly preparing to scale the crags
of those I don't (mostly foreigners). As always, I am deeply impressed by your
range of knowledge and the ease with which you move through literatures that to
me are (literally) closed books.

And please accept my special thanks for the piece you wrote for Anthony's
anthology. Not only was it good of you to take the trouble, but the article itself
delighted me. I had a lot of fun writing those jazz columns, and it is heartening
to have your appreciation, wildly flattering though it is. Such people as have read
the book all pick out your contribution for special mention, as being not only
extremely kind and friendly, and perceptive and witty, but as dealing with the one
book of mine that no one ever bothers about. Who was it who said that age is an
increasing punishment for a crime we have not committed? For me, your article
will be one of the few consolations.

With all good wishes,

Yours ever,

Philip

Philip Larkin to Clive James, 4 May 1982

105 Newland Park
Hull HU5 2DT

5 August 1983

Dear Clive,

Very many thanks for
sending me Brilliant Creatures,
wch gave me a week's cackling.
It took me as long as that
because it's not a book to be
skipped: every sentence had
to be read, unlike those of
— and — and — (especially
her).

But I was late starting
it because my old friend
M. Jones (see dedication of
The Less Deceived) latched onto
it on arrival and wouldn't

Philip Larkin to Clive James, 5 August 1983

let it go, and she was slow
reading it because she is
convalescing from herpes
ophthalmicus, an awful version
of shingles that affects the eye
and makes reading difficult.

'Blake! ... lousy poet and
a lousy artist!' – my heart leapt
up at this, as at so much more.
Of course, this isn't life as I know
it, but I'll take your word for
it, hoping it isn't too much how
you know it. However, at a
Committee I attended on Thursday
a young man arrived bearing
a cycle wheel, so I see some
of it is true anyway. I read
him pp. 253/4.

Again many thanks. I'll
try to send you my Bottom of the Barrel
(collected hackwork) in 'Autumn'. Love S.

An Affair Of Sanity

REQUIRED WRITING BY PHILIP LARKIN

Every reviewer will say that *Required Writing* is required reading. To save the statement from blinding obviousness, it might be pointed out that whereas 'required writing' is a bit of a pun – Larkin pretends that he wouldn't have written a word of critical prose if he hadn't been asked – there is nothing ambiguous about 'required reading'. No outside agency requires you to read this book. The book requires that all by itself. It's just too good to miss.

Required Writing tacitly makes the claim that it collects all of Larkin's fugitive prose, right down to the speeches he has delivered while wearing his Library Association tie. There is none of this that an admirer of his poems and novels would want to be without, and indeed at least one admirer could have stood a bit more of it. The short critical notices Larkin once wrote for the magazine *Listen* are, except for a single fragment, not here. As I remember them, they were characteristically jam-packed with judgements, observations and laconic wit.

If Larkin meant to avoid repetitiveness, he was being too modest: incapable of a stock response, he never quite repeats himself no matter how often he makes the same point. On the other hand there is at least one worrying presence. The inclusion, well-warranted, of the prefaces to *Jill* and *The North Ship* can hardly mean that those books will be dropped from his list of achievements, but the inclusion of the long and marvellous introductory essay to *All What Jazz*, an essay that amounts to his most sustained attack on the modernist aesthetic, carries the depressing implication that the book itself, which never did much business, might be allowed to stay out of print. That would be a shame, because jazz is Larkin's first love and in the short notices collected in *All What Jazz* he gives his most unguarded and exultant endorsement of the kind of art he likes, along with his funniest and most irascible excoriation of the kind he doesn't.

Jazz is Larkin's first love and literature is his first duty. But even at the full stretch of his dignity he is still more likely to talk shop than to talk down, and anyway his conception of duty includes affection while going beyond it, so as well as an ample demonstration of his capacity to speak generally about writing, we are given, on every page of his collection, constant and heartening reminders that for this writer his fellow-writers, alive or dead, are human beings, not abstractions.

Human beings with all their quirks. Larkin proceeds as if he had heard of the biographical fallacy but decided to ignore it. 'Poetry is an affair of sanity, of seeing things as they are.' But he doesn't rule out the possibility that sanity can be hard won, from inner conflict. He has a way of bringing out the foibles of his fellow-artists while leaving their dignity at least intact and usually enhanced. To take his beloved Hardy as an example – and many other examples, from Francis Thompson to Wilfred Owen, would do as well – he convincingly traces the link between moral lassitude and poetic strength. This sympathetic knack must come from deep within Larkin's own nature, where diffidence and self-confidence reinforce each other: the personal diffidence of the stammerer whose childhood was agony, and the artistic self-confidence of the born poet who has always been able to feel his vocation as a living force.

The first principle of his critical attitude, which he applies to his own poetry even more rigorously than to anyone else's, is to trust nothing which does not spring from feeling. Auden, according to Larkin, killed his own poetry by going to America, where, having sacrificed the capacity to make art out of life, he tried to make art out of art instead.

It might be argued that if the Americanised Auden had written nothing else except 'The Fall of Rome' then it would be enough to make this contention sound a trifle sweeping. It is still, however, an interesting contention, and all of a piece with Larkin's general beliefs about sticking close to home, which are only partly grounded in the old anguish of having to ask for a railway ticket by passing a note. He is not really as nervous about Abroad as all that: while forever warning us of the impossibility of mastering foreign languages, he has the right Latin and French tags ready when he needs them, and on his one and only trip to Germany, when he was picking up a prize, he favoured the locals with a suavely chosen quotation in their own tongue.

Lurking in double focus behind those thick specs is a star student who could have been scholarly over any range he chose. But what he chose was to narrow the field of vision: narrow it to deepen it. He isn't exactly telling us to Buy British, but there can be no doubt that he attaches little meaning to the idea of internationalism in the arts. All too vague, too unpindownable, too disrupting of the connections between literature and the life of the nation.

Betjeman was the young Larkin's idea of a modern poet because Betjeman, while thinking nothing of modern art, actually got in all the facts of modern life. Like all good critics Larkin quotes from a writer almost as creatively as the writer writes, and the way he quotes from *Summoned by Bells* traces Betjeman's power of evocation to its source, in memory. The Betjeman/Piper guidebooks, in which past and present were made contemporaneous through being observed by the same selectively loving eye, looked the way Larkin's poetry was later to sound – packed with clear images of a crumbling reality, a coherent framework in which England fell apart. An impulse to preserve which thrived on loss.

In *Required Writing* the Impulse to Preserve is mentioned often. Larkin the critic, like Larkin the librarian, is a keeper of English literature. Perhaps the librarian is obliged to accession more than a few modern books which the critic would be inclined to turf out, but here again duty has triumphed. As for loss, Larkin the loser is here too but it becomes clearer all the time that he had the whole event won from the start.

Whether he spotted the daffodil-like properties of deprivation, and so arranged matters that he got more of it, is a complicated question, of the kind which his critical prose, however often it parades a strict simplicity, is equipped to tackle. Subtle, supple, craftily at ease, it is on a par with his poetry – which is just about as high as praise can go. *Required Writing* would be a treasure house even if every second page were printed upside down. Lacking the technology to accomplish this, the publishers have issued the book in paperback only, with no index, as if to prove that no matter how self-effacing its author might be, they can be even more so on his behalf.

Observer, 25 November 1983

A Valediction
For Philip Larkin

You never travelled much but now you have,
Into the land whose brochures you liked least:
That drear Bulgaria beyond the grave
Where wonders have definitively ceased –
Ranked as a dead loss even in the East.

Friends will remember until their turn comes
What they were doing when the news came through.
I landed in Nairobi with eardrums
Cracked by the flight from Kichwa Tembo. You
Had gone, I soon learned, on safari too.

Learned soon but too late, since no telephone
Yet rings in the wild country where we'd been.
No media penetration. On one's own
One wakes up and unzips the morning scene
Outside one's tent and always finds it green.

Green Hills of Africa, wrote Hemingway.
Omitting a preliminary 'the',
He made the phrase more difficult to say –
The hills, however, easier to see,
Their verdure specified initially.

Fifty years on, the place still packs a thrill.
Several reserves of greenery survive,
And now mankind may look but must not kill

Some animals might even stay alive,
Surrounded by attentive four-wheel-drive

Toyotas full of tourists who shoot rolls
Of colour film off in the cheetah's face
While she sleeps in the grass or gravely strolls
With bloody cheeks back from the breathless chase,
Alone except for half the human race.

But we patrolled a less well-beaten trail.
Making a movie, we possessed the clout
To shove off up green hill and down green dale
And put our personal safety in some doubt
By opening the door and getting out.

Thus I descended on the day you died
And had myself filmed failing to get killed.
A large male lion left me petrified
But well alone and foolishly fulfilled,
Feeling weak-kneed but calling it strong-willed.

Silk brushed with honey in the hot noon light,
His inside leg was colonised by flies.
I made a mental note though wet with fright.
As his mouth might have done off me, my eyes
Tore pieces off him to metabolise.

In point of fact I swallowed Kenya whole,
A mill choked by a plenitude of grist.
Like anabolic steroids for the soul,
Every reagent was a catalyst –
So much to take in sent me round the twist.

I saw Kilimanjaro like the wall
Of Heaven going straight up for three miles.

The Mara river was a music hall
With tickled hippos rolling in the aisles.
I threw some fast food to the crocodiles.

I chased giraffes who floated out of reach
Like anglepoise lamps loose in zero g.
I chased a *mdudu* with a can of bleach
Around my tent until I couldn't see.
Only a small rhinoceros chased me.

The spectral sun-bird drew the mountain near,
And if the rain-bird singing soon soon soon
Turned white clouds purple, still the air was clear –
The radiant behind of a baboon
Was not more opulent than the full moon.

So one more tourist should have been agog
At treasure picked up cheaply while away –
Ecstatic as some latter-day sea dog,
His trolley piled high like a wain of hay
With duty-free goods looted from Calais.

For had I not enlarged my visual scope,
Perhaps my whole imaginative range,
By seeing how that deadpan antelope,
The topi, stands on small hills looking strange
While waiting for the traffic lights to change?

And had I not observed the elephant
Deposit heaps of steaming excrement
While looking wiser than Immanuel Kant,
More stately than the present Duke of Kent?
You start to see why I was glad I went.

Such sights were trophies, ivory and horn
Destined for carving into *objets d'art*.
Ideas already jumping like popcorn,
I climbed down but had not gone very far
Between that old Dakota and the car

When what they told me stretched the uncrossed space
Into a universe. No tears were shed.
Forgive me, but I hardly felt a trace
Of grief. Just sudden fear your being dead
So soon had left us disinherited.

You were the one who gave us the green light
To get out there and seek experience,
Since who could equal you at sitting tight
Until the house around you grew immense?
Your bleak bifocal gaze was so intense,

Hull stood for England, England for the world –
The whole caboodle crammed into one room.
Above your desk all of creation swirled
For you to look through with increasing gloom,
Or so your poems led us to assume.

Yet even with your last great work 'Aubade'
(To see death clearly, did you pull it close?)
The commentator must be on his guard
Lest he should overlook the virtuose
Technique which makes majestic the morose.

The truth is that you revelled in your craft.
Profound glee charged your sentences with wit.
You beat them into stanza form and laughed:
They didn't sound like poetry one bit,
Except for being absolutely it.

Described in English written at its best
The worst of life remains a bitch to face
But is more shared, which leaves us less depressed –
Pleased the condition of the human race,
However desperate, is touched with grace.

The seeming paradox is a plain fact –
You brought us all together on your own.
Your saddest lyric is a social act.
A bedside manner in your graveyard tone
Suggests that at the last we weren't alone.

You wouldn't have agreed, of course. You said
Without equivocation that life ends
With him who lived it definitely dead
And buried, after which event he tends
To spend a good deal less time with his friends.

But you aren't here to argue. Where you are
By now is anybody's guess but yours.
I'm five miles over Crete in a Tristar
Surrounded by the orchestrated snores
Induced by some old film of Roger Moore's.

Things will be tougher now you've proved your point,
By leaving early, that the man upstairs
Neither controls what happens in the joint
We call the world, nor noticeably cares.
While being careful not to put on airs,

It is perhaps the right time to concede
That life is all downhill from here on in.
For doing justice to it, one will need,
If not in the strict sense a sense of sin,
More gravitas than fits into a grin.

But simply staying put makes no one you.
Those who can't see the world in just one street
Must see the world. What else is there to do
Except face inescapable defeat
Flat out in a first-class reclining seat?

You heard the reaper in the Brynmor Jones
Library cough behind your swivel chair.
I had to hear those crocodiles crunch bones,
Like cars compressed for scrap, before the hair
Left on my head stood straight up in the air.

You saw it all in little. You dug deep.
A lesser man needs coarser stimuli,
Needs coruscating surfaces . . . needs sleep.
I'm very rarely conscious when I fly.
Not an event in life. To sleep. To die.

I wrote that much, then conked out over Rome,
Dreamed I'd been sat on by a buffalo,
Woke choking as we tilted down for home,
And now see, for once cloudless, the pale glow
Of evening on the England you loved so

And spoke for in a way she won't forget.
The quiet voice whose resonance seemed vast
Even while you lived, and which has now been set
Free by the mouth that shaped it shutting fast,
Stays with us as you turn back to the past –

Your immortality complete at last.

LRB, 6 February 1986

Getting Larkin's Number

PHILIP LARKIN: A WRITER'S LIFE BY ANDREW MOTION

Somehow serene even in their consuming sadness, beautiful poems made Philip Larkin famous while he was alive. Since his death, ugly revelations threaten to make him more famous still. This unsparing biography furthers the work begun by the *Collected Poems* and the *Selected Letters of Philip Larkin, 1940–1985* of revealing how much more the poor tormented genius had to hide than we ever thought. The mood is catching. By now everybody with something on him is bursting into print. Glumly we learn that he wasn't just a racist, a wanker, a miser and a booze artist, he was also prey, in his declining years, to such nameless vices as conceiving an admiration for Mrs Thatcher.

Larkin often said he wrote poetry out of an impulse to preserve. Unfortunately all who knew him seem to have contracted that same impulse: there is no souvenir they want to forget. The process began when Anthony Thwaite put together a posthumous *Collected Poems* which included all the poems Larkin had so carefully left out of his individual volumes. It was an impressive editorial feat, but the general effect was to blur the universal secret of Larkin's lyricism by putting his personal secrets on display.

The *Letters* continued the process, revealing how thoroughly Larkin could indulge in racism, sexism and all the other -isms when he was trying to shock his unshockable friends. To anyone who knew him, or just knew of him, it was obvious that he was talking that way merely to vent his inner demons: in his public persona he was the soul of courtesy, and until his sad last phase, when his *timor mortis* got the better of him, it was impossible to imagine his being rude or unfair to anyone of any colour, sex or political persuasion.

But to know him is getting harder all the time. Too much information is piling up between the public and the essential man. Andrew Motion has done a meticulous job with this biography but its inevitable effect must be to make the selfless dedication of its hero's work seem self-seeking beyond redemption. Already it is almost too late to point out, for example, that if Larkin made racist remarks in order to be outrageous, then he was no racist. A racist makes racist remarks because he thinks they are true.

Having to argue like this means that the game is lost. No young reader will ever again read Larkin's great tribute to the black jazz musician Sidney Bechet and respond to it with the pure admiration it deserves, since it so exactly registers the equally pure admiration Larkin felt for one of the great men in his life. The most that over-informed new young readers will be able to feel is that the old racist had his decent moments. The possibility will be gone to appreciate that Larkin was a fundamentally decent man; that in his poems he generously shaped and transcended his personal despair to celebrate life on our behalf; and that if he expressed himself unscrupulously in private it was his only respite from the hard labour of expressing himself scrupulously in public.

Still, it is always good to know more, as long as we don't end up knowing less. Here are the details to prove that the picture Larkin painted of himself as a perennial loser didn't necessarily match the way he seemed, even if it was a precise transcription of how he felt. He came up to Oxford as a shy boy with a stammer, but to his fellow undergraduates he was an attractive figure, the kind of wit who makes his friends feel witty too. To the end of his life there were always people eager to crowd around him if he would only let them. Until almost the very end, Larkin was careful not to let them waste his time. He chose his loneliness. Like his diffidence, it was a wish-fulfilment, at odds with the facts.

As a librarian he was a success from the start, rising with each move until, as the guiding light of the Brynmor Jones Library at the University of Hull, he was one of the chief adornments of his profession. Since tact, judgement and self-confidence were necessary at each step, his picture of himself as a ditherer isn't to be trusted. The rabid reactionary turns out to be an equally misleading exercise in self-advertisement. It was on Larkin's instructions that the Brynmor Jones Library built up its Labour Archive, with the Fabian Society Library as chief treasure; now why should a rabid reactionary have done that? Well, one of the answers must surely be that if he felt that way, and even if he talked that way, he didn't actually act that way.

It would certainly help if this possibility could be kept in mind when it comes to the question of women – the only question that really matters to the lifestyle press, whose reporters are currently having a marvellous time patronising Larkin as a lonely, furtive, perverted misogynist utterly unlike themselves. The old women who went as young girls to borrow books from his first library remember him well for his impeccable manners and helpfulness. His first mistress, Ruth Bowman, wrote: 'I'm very proud of you, dear Philip, and I love you very much. The fact that you like me and have made love to me is the greatest source of pride and happiness in my life.' Fifty years later she still remembered him as 'relaxed and cheerful, entertaining and considerate.' At a guess, it was his entertainment value that drew his women in, and his manifest stature as a great artist that kept them loyal through thick and thin.

Admittedly the thin could be very thin. There weren't that many mistresses, but he formed the habit of keeping several on a string at once, so that a few would have looked like a lot if he had wanted to present himself as the Warren Beatty of the literary world. Instead, through his poems and every other available means of communication, he complained endlessly about being rejected by the women he wanted, accepted only by those he didn't, and never getting enough love. This was damned ungallant of him and he was lucky to be forgiven.

It seems he almost always was. The woman to whom he did the most lying, Maeve Brennan, was annoyed enough after she found out to say that she was bitterly disappointed, but apparently still didn't believe that she had wasted her time. Even more convincingly, Monica Jones, to whom he told most of the truth, was there till the end, although the jealousies she suffered along the way must have been almost as great as her love.

Yet his misery was real, and they loved him in spite of it, not because of it. They all had to cope as well as they could with the certain knowledge that he was even more scared of marriage than he was of death. You don't need Freud's help to guess that the primary lesion might have had something to do with his parents. 'They fuck you up, your mum and dad' is clearly one Larkin line that can be taken as what he thought, or at any rate didn't mind having it thought that he thought. Andrew Motion tells us more than we knew before about Dad, who admired the Nazis, although he could scarcely have admired them for helping Germany to achieve its economic recovery in the 1920s (Motion must mean the 1930s). When young Philip confessed his shyness, Dad's reply ('You don't know what shyness is') can't have helped with his son's stammer. He did help, however, with his son's reading: Dad was a well-read man.

On the evidence of this biography, a more likely source of horror at home seems to have been Mum. She could never let go of him or he of her, despite her inability to express herself in anything except platitudes. Mercifully only one fragment of one of her thousands of letters is quoted. It works like one of those revue sketches featuring Terry Jones in a headscarf talking falsetto: 'Here we seem to have a succession of gloomy evenings. It looks as though it will rain again, like it did last night. Have at last heard from Kenneth. He has written such a long and interesting letter thanking me for the handkerchiefs. I have written to thank him . . .'*

Somewhere back there, we can safely assume, lay the source for a feeling of failure that could overcome any amount of success. But finding out more about how Philip Larkin was compelled to solitude can only leave us less impressed by how he embraced it – the most

---

* As the reader will find in the last chapter, I radically changed my estimation of Larkin's mother when more information became available, but it was damned foolish of me to have jumped to the wrong conclusion in the first place.

interesting thing about the man, because it was the key to the poet. It would be obscurantist to want the work of post-mortem explication stopped. But Larkin's executors, in their commentaries, need to be much less humble on his behalf, or else they will just accelerate the growth of this already burgeoning fable about the patsy who has been overpraised for his – we have the authority of Mr Bryan Appleyard on this point – minor poetry.

Andrew Motion has done something to show that Larkin chose the conditions in which to nourish his art, but not enough to insist that art of such intensity demands a dedication ordinary mortals don't know much about. To suggest, for example, that Larkin's last great poem 'Aubade' broke a dry spell of three years is to ignore the possibility that a poem like 'Aubade' takes three years to write, even for a genius. Those who revere Larkin's achievement should be less keen to put him in range of mediocrities who would like to better themselves by lowering him to their level, matching his feet of clay with their ears of cloth.

Independent Sunday Review, 4 April 1993

Postcript to 'An Affair Of Sanity'

To track the closing stages of Larkin's career was among the delights of being a literary critic in the late twentieth century, but the pleasure was not unmixed. Larkin's poetry was, and will always remain, too self-explanatory to require much expounding. Commentary, yes, but explanation no. Puzzle poems like 'Sympathy in White Major' were few, and on the whole his work made a point of declining in advance all offers of academic assistance. So in praising his accomplishment there was always a risk of drawing attention to the obvious. After I tentatively suggested in print that the source of illumination in the central panel of the 'Livings' triptych might be a lighthouse, Craig Raine thrust his impatient face very close to mine and hairily hissed: '*Of course* it's a lighthouse!'* And of course it was. It's all there in the poem, if you look hard enough: and no one else's poetry ever so invited you to look hard and look again.

There was edifying fun to be had, however, in pointing out how Larkin's incidental prose was of a piece with his verse. As a device for self-protection, Larkin was fond of proclaiming his loneliness, misery and bristling insularity, but his prose is there to prove his generous and unprejudiced response to the spontaneous joys of life. With T. S. Eliot, the essay on Marie Lloyd is a one-off: clearly he loved the music hall, but he never contemplated allowing the instinctive vigour of popular culture to climb far beyond the upper basement of his hierarchical aesthetic. Larkin never contemplated anything else. His poem about Sidney Bechet saluted the great saxophonist not just as a master, but as *his* master. For Larkin, pre-modern jazz

* See p. 18.

was the measure of all things: he wanted his poetry to be as appreciable as that. His touchstone for the arts lay in what came to be called the Black Experience.

Helping to make this clear turned out to be useful work, because after his death the scolds moved in. They wanted to dismiss him as a racist, and might have carried the day if a body of sane opinion had not already been in existence. He was also execrated as a provincial, a misogynist and a pornophile. He was none of these things except by his own untrustworthy avowal, usually framed in the deliberately shocking language he deployed in his letters for the private entertainment of his unshockable friends. In his everyday behaviour he did the best a naturally diffident man can to be courteous, responsible and civilised at all times, and in his poetry he did even better than that. In no Larkin poem is there an insensitive remark that is not supplied with its necessary nuances by another poem. To believe Larkin really meant that 'Books are a load of crap' you yourself have to believe that books are a load of crap. The arts pages are nowadays stiff with people who do believe that, even if they think they believe otherwise: all they really care about is the movies. There are people reviewing books, even reviewing poetry, who can read only with difficulty, and begrudge the effort. No writer, alive or dead, is any longer safe from the fumbling attentions of the semi-literate literatus. But here again, the exponential proliferation of bad criticism can scarcely deprive the good critic of a role – quite the contrary. There has to be someone to save what ought to be obvious from the mud-slide of obfuscation, if only by asking such childishly elementary questions as: if you can't see that it took Larkin's personality to produce Larkin's poetry, what can you see? And if you can't accept Larkin's poetry as a self-sustaining literary achievement, what are you doing putting pen to paper?

Reliable Essays, 2001

— This was literally a postscript to the piece when it was republished in *Reliable Essays*, eight years after it was written.

Larkin Treads The Boards

PRETENDING TO BE ME, WRITTEN BY
AND STARRING TOM COURTENAY

Before explaining my belief that Jack Nicholson is the only choice
to play Philip Larkin on screen, I should pay tribute to how well
Tom Courtenay plays him on stage. A one-man show that had the
audience at the Comedy shouting its approval on opening night,
Pretending To Be Me has a booby-trap for a title. When Larkin coined
that phrase, he wasn't saying that he was short of a personality. He
only meant that he didn't want to waste his time, effort and creative
energy on making public appearances to bolster the career of the
famous name he had accidentally become by writing poems quietly
at home. (Now, post mortem, someone else is doing it for him: a
paradox we might have to examine.) Luckily Tom Courtenay, the
principal deviser of the show, is well aware that Larkin, whatever
else he was short of, was never short of a sense of self. If he wound
up as a reclusive curmudgeon, it was a role he chose for himself and
studied with relentless application from quite early on: an act of
assertion if ever there was one. With appropriate decisiveness if
implausible aplomb, Courtenay's Larkin is up there like Judy Garland
at the Palladium. After the third encore, Judy would promise, or
threaten, that the evening wasn't over yet. ('I could sing all night!')
A two-hour monologue from Larkin, all of it drawn from his marvellous prose except when studded with his incomparable poetry: what
could be more riveting? And what could be less likely?

There, of course, lies the show's first and most glaring problem
with verisimilitude. In real life, holding forth at length always rated
high on the list of things Larkin could never be imagined doing. A
weekend in Acapulco with Julie Christie: perhaps yes. But a long
uninterrupted speech? Not a chance. The only reason he would ever

talk for more than two minutes at a stretch was his fear that if you said something he wouldn't understand it. He was deaf. The life that had begun with difficulties in speaking ended with difficulties in hearing. Courtenay retains a hint of the stammer, but uses it as a device for varying the pace and emphasis in a flow of speech that Larkin could never have contemplated. His prose gives us the sense that he could talk like that, but good prose always does, and great prose can almost be defined as the illusion of what can be said concentrated until it sings. Larkin wrote the way he did because he could never talk that way. So the piece rests on an anomaly: reticence on the rampage.

Luckily the theatre, despite Brecht's best efforts, remains a place where we are content to fool ourselves by accepting the patently anomalous. The experimental writer B. S. Johnson once told me that he didn't think Shakespeare's plays were up to much, because real people do not speak poetry. B. S. Johnson is no longer with us, and Shakespeare remains the experimental writer that counts. Similarly, nobody in real life speaks continuously for hours on end unless he is Fidel Castro: but whereas Havana is full of people who wish he wouldn't, and Miami full of people who wish he hadn't, we wish that other people would. Larkin was already near the head of that wish-list before we first-nighters entered the theatre, some of us well armed with memories of every word he had written; but others, presumably, not.

The curtain opened on a set consisting of nothing except a few boxes pretending to be the packed goods Larkin had just moved from one Hull house where he was reasonably content to another Hull house that he hated on sight. Postponing the task of unpacking the 'specially chosen junk' that he once evoked in a poem, he began by speaking prose. Clearly he would speak the prose well. How well he would speak the poetry remained to be heard. The prose was cunningly spliced together from articles, interviews and letters. I could spot nothing that had been posthumously invented for the occasion. This was a mercy, because it would have stood out like a Big Mac at the Last Supper. Courtenay brought to the prose a commendable respect for its tone and rhythm. He varied both without notably distorting either, and apart from a few physical effects he held the attention by the quality of the words alone. (Except for one member of the audience who had attended the event in order to die of diphtheria, there was scarcely a cough all evening.) Admittedly some of Courtenay's physical effects were a bit weird. Prominent among them was his periodic adoption of a wide-legged, knee-trembling, goal-covering stance as if he had suddenly been required to save a penalty from David Beckham. But the only real question about his delivery arose over the poems, and even that question, except at one telling point, was not about the way he spoke them. Last week in this paper Hugo Williams, who had attended a preview, properly raised a general objection to the way actors recite poems. No mean reciter himself, he was well qualified to speak, and he was right. Most actors do bury the rhymes, mangle the rhythms, and comprehensively ruin the poem by trying to put emotion in instead of just contenting themselves with getting it out. But Williams left it politely vague as to whether Courtenay himself was included in this indictment.

I think he should have said specifically that Courtenay wasn't. All of Larkin's poems invite recitation. Even the big poems whose long stanzas would resist being spoken in a single breath always invite you to try. Courtenay was good even with 'The Whitsun Weddings', which is a very hard number to read aloud, because it stretches single sentences over rhymed and rhythmic frames to an extent that Yeats himself, though he pioneered the practice, never pushed quite so far. While making every poem flow like a spontaneous utterance, Courtenay was careful to respect the punctuation, which includes the line-endings, each of them doubling as the phantom comma that a thespian in quest of conversational naturalism typically leaves out. Courtenay's respect for syntax was immaculate, sometimes to the point of pedantry. On the last line of 'An Arundel Tomb' ('What will survive of us is love') he hit the word 'us' as if we who are alive were being contrasted with the figures on the tomb. Professor Ricks has made a case for this possible stressing as part of the last line's putative complexity. But if Larkin had meant that, he would have found a way to stress the point that left less room for Professor Ricks to crash the party. The word to hit is 'survive', because we are being included, along with the effigies, in the contention that our only immortality might consist of a remembered gesture. (The 'might' is covered in the penultimate line: it's only almost an instinctive belief, and it's only almost true.) But an actor who can get your mind working about textual points like that isn't doing too badly, and we can be sure that for listeners coming fresh to Larkin it wasn't the quibbles that mattered: it was the imagery, sent over the footlights like an arrow shower, and right there becoming rain. On the whole Courtenay read the poems better than I ever hoped to hear them read. That wasn't the problem.

The problem with the poems – the second problem of verisimilitude dogging the production – was with the spontaneity, not the utterance. Mercifully never preceded by a drum-roll or postluded by a curtsey for applause, each poem seemed to arise from the surrounding prose, which Courtenay was successfully endeavouring to make sound as if it was being thought up on the spot. The result was that the poems sounded as if they were being thought up on the spot too. If Larkin had been capable of that, either his entire poetic output as we now have it would have been composed in a fortnight, or else he would have spent his lifetime making the torrential Victor Hugo look like the parsimonious Ernest Dowson. But Larkin had to work hard at his craft, and the demands of that work defined his life. In Courtenay's all too accomplished readings, the poetry was respected but the real career, that of poet, was diminished. A poet with Larkin's fanatical standards of quality control must spend a lot of time waiting. Even while he works, he might spend hours trying to fit a single phrase in the right spot. Sometimes Larkin spent decades trying: a long patience. There could be no activity less dramatic, but some attempt might have been made to dramatise it. Courtenay could scarcely have paused for a month or so before reciting each poem. A less impossible device might have been for him to recite one of the poems that Larkin eventually abandoned for want of a single line, and then to supply an appropriate line of prose that might point that fact out. But even in the absence of any means to show the length of time involved in composition, it should have been possible to indicate that the poems had been composed in a way the prose wasn't. (Actually the prose took time too, but much less of it.) Lighting effects are the obvious answer, and at the climactic point, near the end of the show, when Courtenay's recital of the magisterial 'Aubade' marked the oncoming finale of a night out and of a man's life, a lighting effect was actually used. Everything went dark around him, to make him look isolated, instead of just alone.

The upside of this was that one of Larkin's supreme achievements was put in a separate frame. The downside was that Courtenay felt inspired to go for broke. For one almost fatal moment the extraordinary actor became an ordinary actor. Suddenly transforming himself into a human loud-hailer, he ranted a phrase that was begging to be whispered. I won't mention which one it was, because I very much hope that he changes his mind about this initiative, which added colour to the poem only in the way that the uninvited arrival of a circus barker would add colour to a funeral. By then, luckily, the success of the evening was beyond sabotage even from himself. Against all the odds, he had given us the old curmudgeon's tough love of language, the deep secret of his acerbic charm. The question of whether some of the uncharming stuff had been disingenuously left out, however, lingered in the air, even as we stomped and cheered. This was the third problem of verisimilitude, and the one that mattered most.

If some of the critics have been tepid about the show, this problem was their main reason. They have a point. There are cats out of the bag, and Courtenay put them back in. Larkin the pornophile is only fleetingly present, and funny when he is. He complains with disarming bitterness about the way his new television set fails to provide the flood of filth he was threatened with before its purchase, and there is a suggestion that his interest in well-developed schoolgirls might include their corporal punishment. But the pile of treasured top-shelf publications that he might have produced from one of the crates –

just to check that they had not been injured in transit – is not forthcoming. As for his racism, the point is raised only by implication, and solely in his favour. He plays records by Louis Armstrong and Billie Holiday on his obsolescent radiogram, and dances about in silent ecstasy to the music. The implication – and it would have been the right inference to draw – is that the man who was supposed to dislike black people was grateful to black musicians for having made his life more bearable.

But to deal with the point fully would require at least two more elements. One of them would be a recital of his poem 'For Sidney Bechet', in which the great saxophonist is saluted as the exemplar of all joyous creativity, the man of genius to whose eminence Larkin the mere poet can only aspire. No true racist would be capable of such homage. But in fairness to all black Britons who do not play jazz, there would have to be a set of quotations from the bigotry that cropped up in letters he wrote to close friends. I think a fair view of Larkin's prejudices is that he disliked multiculturalism because it altered his bolt-hole version of England, and that he could no more stand alteration than an institutionalised prisoner can stand being issued with a new cup; but there can be no doubt that the way he said so is unpleasant to read, and doubly so because it comes from him. If those remarks were quoted, however, you would also need a disembodied voice to explain that among his circle of unshockable correspondents, to write shocking things was a sport, and that in his public life as a librarian and a literary figure it was unknown for Larkin to be less than courteous to anybody of whatever gender, creed or colour. The disembodied voice, which would need more time on the public address system than Courtenay has on stage, would have to go further, raising the issue of whether or not Larkin made a mistake when he failed to engineer the bonfire of his private papers that he often contemplated. He was an archivist by nature, but he might have foreseen that his impulse to preserve would injure his reputation as a poet after his death. He didn't care about his career in the usual sense of the word, but about his poetic reputation he cared passionately. Yet he would have had to be clairvoyant to guess that his literary executors, by showing us his prejudices, would open the door for a rush of dunces.

The diligence of the executors was perhaps foreseeable. The zeal of the dunces was something else. Invited to attack the man, they have downrated the poet as well, and though the absurdity of this disparagement must eventually become apparent, in the meantime it will serve to ensure that the world's path to the better mousetrap he built becomes an obstacle course. As Hugo Williams noted last week, Bonnie Greer, *per media* the *Mail on Sunday*, recently instructed us to stay cool on the subject. In her view, there was no need to worry about Larkin the racist, because Larkin the poet was not very good anyway. So in her view there was no real problem. Bonnie Greer's sensitivity to poetry could be assessed when she appeared in an episode of BBC 2's *Essential Poems (To Fall In Love With)* and gave her assigned poem the kind of working over calculated to make Hugo Williams take up gardening. Nevertheless, or all the more, she needs to be told that there is a problem after all. Philip Larkin really was the greatest poet of his time, and he really did say noxious things. But he didn't say them in his poems, which he thought of as a realm of responsibility in which he would have to answer for what he said, and answer forever. He also thought there was a temporary and less responsible realm called privacy. Alas, he was wrong about that. Always averse to the requirements of celebrity, he didn't find out enough about them, and never realised that beyond a certain point of fame you not only don't have a private life any more, you never had one. But for treating these themes in *Pretending To Be Me* there is neither time nor room. They would have to be raised in class. Ideally it would be a literature class in which race relations might occasionally be discussed, but the rule of dunces may soon ensure that it will be a race relations class where literature is occasionally discussed, and only as evidence for the prosecution.

On stage, the women who loved Larkin in real life are neither present nor specifically referred to, except perhaps in the beautiful poem about the footprints in the snow, which has recently cropped up even in some of the tabloids, with the addressee duly named and shamed. Normally the tabs are not open to poetry, but all evidence of Larkin's amatory duplicity can now be assured of maximum exposure. This, again, is a huge subject that would be hard to fit on stage even in skeletal form. Just as the man who complained about his shy diffidence was actually an efficient bureaucrat at the top of his profession, the man who complained so often about missing out on love was actually surrounded by it. If Larkin was not exactly Warren Beatty, he certainly bore, in his multiple liaisons if not in his personal appearance, a striking resemblance to Albert Camus. In the week before Camus met his death in a suitably glamorous car-crash, he wrote to five different women pledging eternal fealty to each, and he was probably telling the truth every time. Larkin had a similar network of affectionate loyalties, but always with the proviso that his life had to remain undivided. Not even Monica Jones, who was the closest to being a companion, got a share of his solitude. When he said 'Deprivation is for me what daffodils were for Wordsworth' he left open, beyond the simple statement, the complex implication that if he had not been granted sufficient deprivation he would have had to seek more of it. The play depends on the assumption that the life shaped the work. The proposition that the work shaped the life would be too difficult to discuss in the theatre, and would be hard enough to discuss for a panel of professors locked up together for a year. If we accept all these limitations as inevitable, *Pretending To Be Me* can be hailed for what it is. It gives us a bravura performance by an actor who understands that bravura must be in service to emotion, and not just a display of technique. It shows a curmudgeon doing what curmudgeons do best: being sardonically funny about life. Above all it brings to the theatre the primal exultation of language; the very thing that has made the English theatre thrilling since Mercutio first told Romeo about Queen Mab; the thing from which it can stray only so far before ceasing to be substantial.

The only question now is who will play Larkin next. Courtenay can't keep it up forever: for only one set of vocal cords, the piece must be like trying to sing the whole of *Aida* on your own. The perfect lookalike, Eric Morecambe, is sadly not available, and anyway he was too merry. Alexei Sayle could do it: he's the wrong shape, but he can do the right kind of humour, which is the curmudgeon's humour, and thus not very merry at all, because it makes jokes about the world falling apart only on the understanding that the man making them is falling apart as well.

Recasting the leading role in your own mind is a good sign: it means you think the script is alive. Recasting it for Hollywood is a bigger challenge, but it will have to be faced. Courtenay has been a fine film actor at every stage of his career (if you think nothing could be better than his appearance in *Billy Liar*, see him in *The Dresser*) but Miramax will probably want an American. Miramax won't relocate Larkin from Hull to Harvard: Harvey Weinstein knows by now that British literary life has a solid appeal on the art-house circuit and a pipeline to the Oscars. But Weinstein will want a bankable star. According to my own sources, Robert De Niro has already declared his interest, but to prepare himself for the role he wants to spend fifty years in a library. Bruce Willis wants the library to be taken over by terrorists. Seriously, it has to be Jack Nicholson. Jack has been in training as a curmudgeon since the campfire scene in *Easy Rider*. Remember *Five Easy Pieces*? 'Hold the mayo.' The scorn, the bitterness! Nobody does sardonic better. There is nobody like him for disillusioned. When Jack gives it the bared teeth and the arched eyebrows, he could recite his own death sentence and still sound funny.

The beauty part is that Jack just played an irascible old bastard and will probably get an Oscar for it. In *About Schmidt* he's Philip Larkin without the bifocals. Admittedly Schmidt doesn't write poetry or do anything very much. The movie, which you should see unless you have a chance to visit a molasses factory, asks us to believe that Schmidt has wasted his life in an insurance office. But since there is no residual evidence of any personal qualities that he might have wasted, Jack is left to convey little except an unspecific sense of having achieved nothing. To put it another way, he is left to convey nothing. He does this by impersonating a stunned mackerel with a comb-over. But at least there are no mannerisms. Jack is ready to begin again, after Stanley Kubrick set him on the wrong track by convincing him that there could be an acting style beyond naturalism. There is no acting style beyond naturalism except ham, as Jack proved in *Prizzi's Honor*, where he pioneered his latter-day schtick of clenching his lips with difficulty over an object he was reluctant to identify. By the time he got to *As Good As It Gets*, you would have thought he was concealing a live mouse in his mouth. But when he bared his teeth at Helen Hunt like a wolf with its eye on a new-born lamb, we got a reminder of what this man could do, and can still do. That killer drawl is ready for its greatest workout. And he only wants a few changes. 'Your mom and pop, heh heh. They fuck you over, right?' Coming soon to a multiplex near you.

TLS, 28 February 2003

Postscript

Ian McEwan said that he would never forgive me for having written this piece, because it persuaded him to break his personal rule of staying away from the theatre. Choosing his words with care, he told me that he had disliked the evening very much, and that he thought me demented, if not criminal, for having encouraged people into the theatre with my review, instead of standing outside the theatre and encouraging them to go home. Speaking as one who loved Larkin's poetry at least as much as I did, he wanted to know how I could be a party to a theatrical presentation that might have been designed specifically to render the poetry less meaningful, by promoting the idea that such a concentration of emotion needed acting out. I tried to tell myself that Courtenay's performance might have gone off a bit since I first saw it, but on second thoughts I had to admit that McEwan might have had at least the ghost of a point. Hadn't I, while watching the play, been thinking that it would be a good introduction to Larkin's poetry for young people who had never read it? And hadn't I, who knew his work well, also been thinking that to hear even the best actor read the words aloud was nothing like as good as becoming acquainted with them in the silence of print? In other words, I had been thinking of what might be good for others: a sure-fire formula for distorting one's initial response. But my first thoughts were the ones I wrote down in that same week, and I was glad to have done so. One young lady said that my review led her to the play, that the play led her to Larkin, and that his poetry became part of her life. She recited the last lines of 'Dockery and Son' to prove it. There had to be something good about that chain of events, at a time when accredited arts experts were lining up in print, on radio and on television to insist that the old fool had never been worth bothering with.

Now it can be revealed: the phrase of 'Aubade' that Courtenay hammered was 'This one will', and it had the effect of dropping a mortar bomb into the adagio of Schubert's C major string quintet. The anomalous uproar was especially unfortunate because 'Aubade' is the poem that so many of Larkin's literary admirers think of when they hear the creaking of death's door. 'Aubade' unites other writers in a common worship. People agree about its quality who agree about nothing else. Harold Pinter can recite the whole poem from memory while seated at the dinner table. The poem is a point of reference in Simon Gray's *The Smoking Diaries*. Very few poems have that kind of currency. Tom Courtenay probably thought the same: the reason that he gave it special treatment. He should have copied Pinter, who dials down the histrionics. But finally the poem outclasses even the most beautiful voice that tries to recite it. One is reminded of what Schnabel said about Beethoven's late piano sonatas: music better than can be played.

The Meaning of Recognition, 2005

Life, Art, Love, And Like That

In 2014 I was invited by the *New York Times Book Review* to write a piece about the soon-to-be published American edition of James Booth's biography of Larkin. Though I was short of puff by then, I took the assignment because the book-reviewing process in America runs more slowly and simply than it does in Britain (you practically have to quote a few lines of Shakespeare to back up your contention that he was a poet), so you get a chance to sum up a long-running controversy at a decently non-hectic pace. The Americans don't always react well to the suggestion that a poet might sometimes not mean what he says. If you think they should, however, you have to ask yourself why you are so keen to sell them a tricky book.

PHILIP LARKIN: LIFE, ART AND LOVE – BY JAMES BOOTH
REVIEWED BY CLIVE JAMES

James Booth's new biography of Philip Larkin is not very exciting, perhaps because James Booth has the sense to leave the exciting writing to Larkin. But it is very welcome. If you believe that Larkin wrote some of the best English-language poems of modern times, then it has been a trial to see his questionable track record as an everyday human being get in the way of his reputation as an artist.

The obfuscation happened in a hurry, only a few short years after Larkin died in 1985. His pair of distinguished literary executors, Anthony Thwaite and Andrew Motion, served him faithfully with a selection of his letters (edited by Thwaite) and a biography (written by Motion). Unfortunately for Larkin's image, it became evident that he had indulged himself in racist and sexist language. It had not occurred to the executors that they might have prefaced their respective volumes with a health warning in capital letters pointing out what should have been obvious: that Larkin talked that way only in his private life; that he believed his letters to be part of his private life too; and that in his public life he was courteous and charming to anyone he met, of whatever gender or racial background.

Plainly they hadn't thought it necessary. It shouldn't have been. But there were dunces waiting, who relished the chance to diminish him. A depressing number of British literary figures averred that it was no longer necessary to read Larkin's poetry, and a few of them were dumb enough to say that it had never been any good in the first place.

This reversal of estimation was too wild to stick. There were too many people – on both sides of the Atlantic, and anywhere else where English is read and spoken – who simply loved his poems. In the last two decades that opinion has managed to reassert itself: an encouraging example of error wearing out its welcome. The chief virtue of Booth's new book, then, is not to advance a new opinion, but to sensibly demonstrate why the original opinion remains the opinion that matters.

Booth is an excellent guide to just why a Larkin poem can merit being called great. He points out its features with the proud care of a well-suited senior BMW executive taking a turn in the salesroom. He is sensitive enough not only to praise the master at his best but to spot the moments when his sublime talent is not fully engaged. Towards the end, Larkin tried to repeat the tone and message of his mighty poem 'The Whitsun Weddings' by composing a similarly exalted hymn to traditional social values called 'Show Saturday'. Unfortunately, despite its typical care for detail and craft of assembly, 'Show Saturday' is burdened with language that does not sing. Booth uses exactly the right word: 'listless'. (p 387)

Booth's limiting estimation of 'Show Saturday' counts as good critical sense, and thus serves to offset the strange moment when he counts the famous second-last line of 'An Arundel Tomb' – 'Our almost-instinct almost true' – among Larkin's 'awkward felicities'. (p116) Booth forgets to say that the line is really about as un-awkward as a felicity can get. But Booth has not really written an academic book. He has written a book of the higher journalism, which is still the kind of attention Larkin needs: although from now on, and partly due to Booth's book, he might need it less. The way will now be open for commentators on this most lyrically rich of modern poets to be as tin-eared as they like.

Booth, in his own prose, is only occasionally deaf to rhythm. 'He was not yet prepared to throw in the poetic towel' is a construction apt to induce a pain in the critical neck. (p394) But the sentence only limps, it doesn't just lie there and blow bubbles. More importantly, Booth has a good ear for Larkin's real-life speech. When Larkin helped to finance the publication of his first major collection *The Less Deceived* by agreeing that it be sold by subscription, he privately called the subscribers 'the sucker list'. (p203) But he was joking, and one of the many merits of Booth's book is that he can spot Larkin's jokes. Larkin spoke and wrote the allusive, indirect and ironic tongue of the British literary world. In a time which grows more literal-minded almost as fast as it grows less literary, a tongue in the cheek will always need translating, especially to Americans, who expect straightforward honesty, and tend to find all obliquity duplicitous. And indeed there were times when Larkin imitated the action of the weasel.

Larkin was a model of probity in his professional lives as a writer and a librarian, but in his love life he was not honest. The uncovering of his cover-ups is by now probably complete, although in view of his ability to attract women – an ability that he made such a point, in his poetry, of saying he lacked – it won't be much of a surprise if a couple more turn up. With two conspicuous exceptions, the women we know about were reticent and conventional: normally they would not have done such a not-done thing as form a liaison with a colleague, but Booth points out persuasively that their quiet lives, so short of excitement, might have been the exact reason why they couldn't resist the charm of his company. He spoke well.

Whether, lacking the hit rate of his handsome friend Kingsley Amis, Larkin was any great shakes after he had got them into bed is something most of us have been inclined to doubt until now, if only on the evidence of his poetry, which places great emphasis on his being left out of the sexual adventure. But one of the conspicuous exceptions, the semi-bohemian academic Monica Jones, was certainly keen to do anything for him when it came to the boudoir. Even more convincingly, the other conspicuous exception, Patsy Strang – an experienced vamp with no patience for a merely spiritual relationship – was crazy about him until the end of her life, and long after their love affair was over she turned up begging for him to take her back. That kind of evidence doesn't make him Errol Flynn, but it does put a damper on his image as a chump.

Perhaps pretending to be a sexual non-starter was part of his strategy. In the animal world, stealthy diffidence is sometimes a useful lead-up to a deadly leap. If so, it was one more deception, in the one area of his life where he really had something to be ashamed of. The man who said such beautiful things in tribute to black musicians couldn't really have been race-prejudiced even if he claimed to be. But the man who hid his women from one another was causing real damage, because some of them – and those the shyest, nicest and most decent – spent years being led up the garden path. It was cruel of him. Perhaps he just hated the idea of hurting them. Anyway, hurt them he did, a sad fact which Booth is ready to face. But he is also ready to face the even sadder fact that it took Larkin's injured psyche to produce the serene poems at which we now murmur in astonishment, mouthing the beautiful phrases as we read.

New York Times Book Review, 22 November 2014

Philip Larkin: Letters Home
1936–1977

As the ancillary books of correspondence and commentary accumulate, our picture of Philip Larkin grows more nuanced all the time, and at this rate he will soon be as complex a character as your batso uncle, the one who thought that modern society was falling apart for lack of discipline. This new collection of *Larkin's Letters Home* from 1936 to 1977 does a vital job of apprising us, if we ever thought the opposite, that his father's pre-war admiration for the Nazis stopped well short of staging a Nuremberg rally in the parlour, and that his mother, while undoubtedly prey to psychological frailties, was no dullard. On page 483, near the end of the book, she can be found reading *The Rainbow*, but firm in her opinion that *Sons and Lovers* was its superior.

Larkin himself is only fifty at the time, but his famously febrile mother, born in 1886, is the full eighty-plus years of age including mandatory doddering. Yet on page 490 one of her letters mentions Hardy, Lamb and Hazlitt. We learn that Larkin's father, as famous for being pro-Nazi as his wife is for being feeble-minded, had every book by Lawrence, all in a row, and yet on page 568 we find, *per contra*, that he is a fan of *Howards End*. Why do I suddenly have such trouble imagining Larkin senior dressed up as Baldur von Schirach, the Nazi Youth leader who composed a formally impeccable *terza rima* panegyric to Hitler?

Perhaps the neurotic pallor of Larkin's upbringing was more nuanced than we thought. If that possibility could be entertained, it might be a help towards realising that the mentality of one of the most subtle and inventive of modern creative lives didn't come out of nowhere. There was history behind it: his history, his family's history, and finally our history too. There was an arrow shower, somewhere becoming rain.

At some time in the future after he had committed the arrow shower to paper, the poet let on that he had got it from Olivier's movie of *Henry V*. Most of us needed no telling: the poetic moment and the cinematic coup were so similar in their intensity. How a critic as finely tuned as Al Alvarez could ever have thought Larkin's poetry was overly genteel is a secret that Alvarez, old and ill now, will probably take with him into silence: but we can confidently say that Larkin's verses had an awful lot of dynamism for a critic to miss spotting. (I doubt if Alvarez did miss spotting it, actually, but he was misled by his fond theory that poetry should exact a psychological cost from the poet, and Robert Lowell's berserk stare made the gleam in Larkin's glasses look placid.)

In actuality, Larkin could see everything. Even the effigies on the Arundel tomb – he with his hand withdrawn from its gauntlet, so as to hold her hand – are moving at the speed of the light that throngs the glass, the same speed as all the things we see in the everyday world are moving into the future. The clouds above the estuary stand still only on the understanding that the earth spins and the sun that lights them moves through space. To think that Larkin has not incorporated all this universal energy into his poetic rhythms is to imitate the action of the clod.

Speaking for myself, in my recent role as a frail old man, Larkin's verbal dynamism still tears me to bits. My granddaughter, who jumps everywhere like an ecstatic wallaby, jumps in just the way that his enchanted Alice jumped more than half a century ago, when I first read *The Less Deceived*, a little book that did so much to teach a generation how the next world happens here, where we live now. Larkin could deal in exaltation because he knew despair; and you didn't have to read him for long before realising that he might be stoking the despair in order to further illuminate the exaltation. His career as a poet was a brilliant job of titrating his own propensities. If I could meet him again I might dare to tell him so but you had to be careful how you praised him: when his projection mechanism was set to self-deprecation he didn't necessarily like to be interrupted. He might even have been sincerely worried when he warned his parents that Oxford was going to give him a third-class degree. In fact it gave him a first.

With a pause to consider the likelihood that his parents must have been well used to it ('I don't believe that your writing is "not any good", as you put it' his supposedly infirm mother says firmly on page 565), this habit of self-belittlement needs to be borne in mind whenever he says he hates his job as a librarian. Invariably he did it as if he loved it. There was no duty, even when self-imposed, that he would not complain about in his writings – even in his poems, the celebrations usually begin as laments – but equally there was no duty that he would ever skimp. A pose of bitching unease was part of his compliance. As often as not, his attitudes of irritated revulsion were components in a strategy of staving off the world's enchantment. The 'loaf-haired secretary' might have looked like Julie Christie.

As a poet and a man of letters, Larkin is bottled lightning: the man who can say it so that it stays said. Who else do we want him to be? Stewart Granger in the striped tights of Scaramouche? Captain Marvel? The Man from Snowy River? For decades now it's been damned foolish of us to be so fascinated by his faults, when we've barely made a start on appreciating his virtues. And anyway, as we should well know by now, most of his faults were cried up by himself as a polite kind of negative self-publicity. The transformative qualities of his vision – the qualities that make the cloudscape above the estuary into a baroque gallery – are the very qualities that make him an unreliable witness to his quotidian feelings. When talking about how he detests his room and its specially chosen junk, the operative word is 'chosen': hidden in plain sight, the junk adds up to an affirmation of his freedom. In correspondence – especially when the correspondent was Kingsley Amis – Larkin enjoyed making himself out as someone prejudiced against black people. But he also wrote the greatest ever poem in praise of Sidney Bechet, and in *All What Jazz* – one of the great books of creative criticism in our language – the black musicians are celebrated as if arriving by the heroic ship-load on the beach at Troy. Surely the best way to deal with this anomaly is to say, truly, that Larkin's poems were for the public, whereas he thought his letters were private.

In that respect – and, to my mind, in that respect alone – the monumentally great man was a gibbering dunce. To attest a racial prejudice in such publishable form would have been folly even when Victoria was Queen, and for a librarian, of all professions, to do so throughout the reign of the second Elizabeth was simply asking for it. He was lucky that she, when conferring his CBE, asked him only whether he was 'still writing'. He could have answered, truthfully, that he was working on a tiny epic called 'Aubade' that would help define his era and hers, but he was probably anticipating the nudge from Pursuivant Usher in Waiting that meant 'Start walking backwards now'.

Nevertheless it was a close shave. If his letters had already been published he would have found for certain that publicly expressed bigotry was infra dig. Robert Mugabe was asked to dinner at the palace but he was a black African and therefore presumably licensed to kill other black Africans by the thousand: a mere British librarian would never have made it, and might even have had his laureateship withdrawn. (As it happened, or failed to happen, the laureateship was never conferred, but only because he refused it.) Once his playful prejudice was out there in print, it ceased to be playful, and there is no joy to be had from it even now. There was almost no racial group of any size or colour that he could not be prejudiced about in a letter, but it can't be denied that there was something twisted about the way he got his xenophobic rocks off in private: it was almost a perversion that the same man who could go on building up the collection of Labour Party documents at the Brynmor Jones Library could believe that his own words – words, his best thing, the thing for which he must have known that he was already cherished – would be forgotten.

But you need to be even sillier than he was to deduce that his poetry was, as a consequence, no good. I knew a prominent

Cambridge female don, a close friend of our family, who announced that opinion at the top of her voice, and I spent a lot of time with my hand over my eyes, as a polite alternative, I thought, to sticking my fingers in my ears. My chief reservation about the diligent curative work of Anthony Thwaite and Andrew Motion, the two poets who laid the foundations of Larkin's posthumous outline – Thwaite getting the poems together, and Motion telling the biographical story that lay behind them – is how they played into the lady's hands by not pointing out often enough that Larkin's private life was a sideshow; that his poetry, along with its attendant literary activities, was his real life; and that anyone who couldn't grasp that fundamental fact shouldn't be talking about him at all, lest they leave his true heritage at the mercy of tin-eared misrepresentation.

This last thing was exactly what happened, and we're still coming out if it. The lady I was talking about is gone now, but Tom Paulin, for example, is still alive and kicking, and until he tells us otherwise we must assume that he is still kicking Larkin. On that subject, the suave, saturnine and velvet-voiced Paulin has always needed to look into a mirror and realise the extent to which he has not been handicapped even by his blessings. As a poet, Paulin looks the part. When Larkin looked into a mirror he saw an impostor.

At least one of Larkin's numerous female admirers (contrary to his own self-generated publicity, he was unsuccessful with women in the same way that Pete Sampras was unsuccessful at Wimbledon) thought and said that to be granted his attention was the greatest thing that ever happened to her in her life, but in this matter Larkin was not to be dissuaded by reality. All the accumulating evidence might confirm the supposition that women fall in love through the ears, not through the eyes, but as a matter of disposition he was well protected against romantic beguilement. Monica Jones was clearly indispensable to him and speculators have wondered why, as if it were a mystery; but they haven't thought sufficiently hard about the way he wanted to hear her opinions about a new poem, and often enough, would accept her suggestions. Kingsley Amis loathed her and even his son Martin, a more tolerant soul at every level, found her hard to take, but the point remains that Larkin couldn't do without her opinion. Those who deride her for her lack of academic achievement – not a single publication in a learned journal: how can such things be? – are apt to forget that her critical scrutiny was vital to a great poet and is therefore implicitly present in a whole swathe of his finest work stretching from year to year: another corridor of light in the palace of cloud above the estuary. On top of that, she helped him, at his request, make a bonfire of his journals, which might have been her most creation-friendly assisting act of all, when you consider what a dog's breakfast was almost immediately made of his incidental heritage. In his role as a supreme literary figure, the last thing he needed was more old rope to hang himself with.

Those of us who laugh aloud at Monica's stridently nutty incarnation as Margaret Peel in *Lucky Jim* are apt to neglect her spectral presence in *The Whitsun Weddings* and a dozen other of the most magnificent poetic achievements since Donne and Marvell, but the fault is Larkin's when it is not ours. He felt compelled to emphasise that he was alone, and perhaps to acknowledge Monica would have been like lavishing too much praise on his mother for her choice of sponge cake. Dante might have felt the same when he left his wife out of his biggest poem and directed all the love-stuff towards Beatrice. Yeats in his swan-song years sinned in the same way every time he sang. From now until doomsday, scholars will argue about whether or not great artists construct their own personalities in order to fulfil their fate, but surely the only true answer adds up to a double-yolked egg of rhetorical questions: 'Why ever not?' and 'Who cares?'

Larkin's real imposture was as someone who found the banal even more banal than we do. But from this book it can soon be deduced that in his regular, sedulously uneventful letters to his mother he was not talking down to her, he was restoring his supply of the precious ordinariness that she represented. Critics and commentators have gone on for years failing to realise, even as their hair grows thin, that they themselves have never led the life of James Bond, and that they should therefore be slower to find it boring when the great poet and his almost equally non-glamorous mother get into a dialogue about the new M&S line in preserved peaches. In such exchanges, Larkin was probably just as much instigator as supplicant. When he needed the sublime he could read great literature, but to catch the more nuanced tones of everyday life he needed agents out there among the supermarket shelves, and in that respect his mother was a wizard. After burying the parachute she could blend with the local population in a trice.

Even within those parameters, he still found room for the occasional almost Kingsley-like gag: having eaten out on the night before he writes to her, he complains of the 'turf-like salmon, . . . fried in engine oil'. But mainly he wasn't out to entertain her with comic brilliance: he was out to share her involvement in the detail and texture of ordinary reality.

On that last point, I can recommend without reserve the action sequence on page 533 where he tells her about painting his house-number on the new dustbins. There are critics, and there are even scholars, who seem convinced that he would have been a more interesting man if, while painting the bins, he had been targeted from the air by a SPECTRE attack helicopter with Ernst Stavro Blofeld at the controls ('No, Mister Larkin, I expect you to die!'), but instead he was dedicated to writing poems.

Dedicated or condemned? The question turns on that distinction. But to think him condemned, you have to believe what he says when he's not writing poetry, and the simple truth is that you almost always can't. In prose, he would talk for effect, and usually at the exact level of his interlocutor. Occasionally, even when writing to his mother – the most experienced interlocutor of them all, even more so than Monica Jones – his guard slips and he lets the other world, the poetic world, punch through. This from page 253:

> ' . . . I went out to the local branch library to change my books
> & was overwhelmed by the soft beauty of the afternoon . . .
> outside my own miserable cramped absurd life, the world is still
> its old beautiful self. This morning the sun shines . . .'

I break off at that moment with confidence that you will be able to imagine what he tells her next. Blofeld's helicopter diving to the attack, as part of the master villain's plan to destroy the future of British poetry? Or, more likely, the long exchange about the ideal size of teacup is resumed. Either way, what we need to grasp is that the master poet didn't necessarily find anything less marvellous just because it was always there. The sun, for example, was still up there being its beautiful self.

Mind you, he could be strange. (Voice of God: 'You think he was strange? Wait till I introduce you to Michelangelo.') Considering the immense trouble it must have taken to write *Trouble at Willow Gables*, I myself was inclined to think its author, at least while he was hatching that one, was a nut. It was the way it wasn't pornographic that staggered me. These infants were in paradise, but from what boiling, twisting psychic ambivalence came all that finely noticed detail about a world without men? Well, now we know: he was channelling his mother. Far from being particularly bent, he was cashing in on his Royal Box ticket to an operatic layout by which women not only crowded the stage, they shared the leading roles. Only by historic accident can this be taken as a perennial inhibition, a sign of imprisonment in an ambivalent mentality. In actuality, it was a vision of heaven. Eventually, no matter how cloddish we might personally be, if we listen closely enough we will see what he is really a victim of: the world, its vividness. We will even figure out why his accounts of the schoolgirls playing hockey have the specificity of Pope's cataloguing of Belinda's dressing table in *The Rape of the Lock*. We will figure out everything except precisely where the girls, whether sprinting on the field or lolling at its edge, got their tanned bare legs from. Bare, yes; but tanned? Come on, this is a dream England, with its set-dressing suggestion of floor-level sun-lamps.

And eventually even those conjured young females – the yearning poet's *jeunes filles en fleur* – grew old. The Old Fools: why aren't they screaming? As an old fool myself these days, and often enough laid up in hospital when not being pampered here at home, I'm prepared to say that there's a working TV set in both locations and perhaps the reason the old fools aren't screaming is because they've just been watching Ernie Wise dance, and found his self-delighted, light-footed élan as enchanting as Eric's jokes. Right there was a point I would have loved to discuss with Larkin. But I wasn't smart enough – or wasn't yet sick enough – to know that we can get very near the end and still be thankful to have lived. He would have said otherwise, but you couldn't trust him.

Prospect, December 2018

Coda

In whatever month of whatever year – anyway, about fifty years ago – Pete Atkin and I were doing what we thought would be our last tour of the country to promote our most recent album of songs, and one of the venues was the Student Union bar at Hull University. We didn't know at the time that our songs, mainly thanks to YouTube, would one day be back in business, so the occasion could have been funereal. But the joint was jammed. Among those jamming it, I eventually noticed, was a tall figure looming at the back of the room. Before the end of the show, I'd realised it was Philip Larkin, and wondered why a deaf man should have come to hear us perform. Among the students he looked like a plain-clothes policeman among vagrants.

After the lights came up, I asked him why he was there, and he told me that although he couldn't hear very well, he had been keen to find out what exactly I was doing. I think it was the idea of going public in such a blatant way that fascinated him, or perhaps appalled him. I can remember him saying that he didn't pretend to be interested in any sort of popular music except pre-modern jazz, but he was intrigued that I thought poetry could be popular entertainment. He couldn't imagine himself standing up to perform, while I couldn't imagine myself not doing so.

Later on, I realised that his attendance at our show had been one of the great compliments I'd been paid in my life. At the time, I was too young, and too obtuse, to understand that he was a busy man, with every hour of every day spoken for. I knew he was famous, and thought, even then, that he was deservedly so. He was, as yet, far from writing and publishing 'Aubade', but there was something about him that was already saying goodbye.

I was left with the impression of a generous and courteous man. This impression was confirmed several times by letters which were kindly interested in their recipient's welfare, even while he himself was ill, and, finally, dying. He was a gentleman, and his gentleness was something he was trying to offset when his poetry was savage.

This book is a gathering of all the times I felt compelled to register my admiration for his work. And even in the times between, his books were always within reach, especially when his detractors were closing in. The critical focus is, often now, so exclusively about his personal failings. I felt the need to add here, at the end, this reminiscence of his decency and politeness. Old-fashioned virtues indeed, as he would no doubt have been dryly aware.

The University of Hull
The Brynmor Jones Library

Librarian: Professor P.A. Larkin, C.H., C.B.E., C.Lit., M.A., D.Lit., D.Litt., F.R.S.L., F.L.A., F.R.S.A.

PAL/LT

15th August, 1985

Clive James, Esq.,
536 Willoughby House,
The Barbican,
LDONDON EC2

Dear Clive,

    Many thanks for your kind letter of 10th July; I am only now
beginning to grapple with my accumulated correspondence. Yes, it
has been a rotten few months, but I am at home convalescing now, and
am assured of ultimate recovery. Can't say I feel much like it yet,
but this is 'quite normal at this stage'.

    I shall greatly look forward to your next instalment of
autobiography. I suppose I ought to be doing something like that,
while the machine is still to me, but I can only sit in a chair
and dictate inadequately to my invaluable secretary who takes away,
types and sends. This does not mean that the gratitude they convey
is any less sincere.

               Yours ever,

               Philip

Postcode: HU6 7RX   *Telephone:* 0482 46311   *Telex:* 592530 UNIHUL G

Philip Larkin to Clive James, 15 August 1985.
The phrase 'while the machine is still to me', meaning
'while I still have life and breath', echoes Hamlet's letter to Ophelia
(as read by Polonius) in Act 2, Scene 2 of Hamlet.